The Marriage of All and Nothing

... when I found him
whom my soul
loves;
I held him and
would not let him go.

The Song of Songs
3 : 4

The Marriage of All and Nothing:

Selected Writings of Barbara Dent

Edited by Mary Freiburger

6/19/09

Your longing echoes my desire for You.

ICS Publications
Washington, D.C.
2002

May your Spirit, O Jesus, be the only rule of my life.

ICS Publications
2131 Lincoln Road NE
Washington DC 20002-1199

ACKNOWLEDGMENT

Those responsible for the following publications have agreed to
reprinting materials that originally appeared in their periodicals:

Cross and Crown (discontinued in 1992)
Desert Call
Mount Carmel
New Zelandia
Review for Religious
Spiritual Life

Library of Congress Cataloging-in-Publication Data

Dent, Barbara
  The marriage of all and nothing: selected writings of Barbara Dent;
edited by Mary Freiburger.
  p. cm.
ISBN 0-935216-26-X
I. Spiritual life—Catholic Church. I Freiburger, II Title.
BX2350.2 .D4467 2000
242—dc21   00-058048

Contents

Preface

After successful distribution of Barbara Dent's *My Only Friend is Darkness* over several years, ICS Publications is glad to offer a set of selected articles already published elsewhere but now difficult to find, complemented by forty-one unpublished poems.

The New Zealand author's intensely personal, lived-through style gives "flesh and bones" to the notion of the "dark night of the soul" in this new book. We are grateful to Barbara Dent for going beyond generic or generalized expositions of that key concept of Carmelite spirituality, to craft her own vivid witness that speaks always in tones of our times. She accurately describes the contemporary scene as "an age of change, bewilderment, confusion, and contradiction" (p. 73). She proves she is a child of this same age by using contemporary terms like "a piece of lost luggage" (62), "confetti at nuptials" (71), "power failure" (116), "nuclear holocaust" (211), and many others. This she does as a mother, writer, poustinik, and Carmelite secular order member.

Particularly interesting is the way she identifies the major events of her adult life in biographical pieces, both in prose and in poetry, allowing us to appreciate how adept a guide she is to managing the darkness of physical suffering and spiritual progress. She does not hesitate to cite perennially valid terms such as "holy indifference," so as to draw on the wisdom of past masters, but she knows how to weave them into an overall narrative that demonstrates her own special "creative fidelity" to an ongoing

Christian mystical tradition. Readers are sure to appreciate all the attention she pays, in line with modern renewal movements, to the resurrection as an integral part of spiritual development.

We are indebted to her American agent Mary Freiburger, for her assistance in assembling the typescript from its various sources. Fr. Steven Payne, finishing an assignment in Africa at a regional study house of our Order, deserves appreciation for the work he devoted to preparing this volume for publication.

Fr. John Sullivan, OCD
Publisher

Introduction

I came to know Barbara Dent and her writing through a friend who had been writing to her for assistance in his spiritual journey. At his request, I wrote Barbara to inform her how I saw his journey from my perspective as his director. Her reply demonstrated spiritual depth and wisdom, and she asked me perceptive questions about how I was walking with my friend. I answered her and thus began our exchange over the past five years. At one point Barbara wrote that she did not have a spiritual director, and would I consider being her spiritual guide by mail. I hesitated to do so because of the advanced state of her spiritual experience. Her response was, "If you can counsel one who is in the dark night of the soul, why do you hesitate with me?" We began almost weekly exchanges, and Barbara opened her soul to me, and I saw one much loved by God. What became apparent almost from the beginning was that we viewed the spiritual life in much the same way—the way of positive surrender to the will of God in all things, the way of loving obedience to the Father by the obedience of the Son living in us.

Then, Barbara wrote to say that a brain tumor had been diagnosed and she could die at any time. My directee friend and I both felt moved to visit her in New Zealand while she was still reasonably well. I secured the proper permissions, and we arrived at her poustinia near Auckland in February, the warm summer weather being a sharp and welcome contrast to the winter I had left home in Canada.

We had Mass in her home each morning. Barbara tired very easily and was not well, yet I came to know her firsthand as a woman, as a directee, and as a writer. She was happy when we discussed the life of faith. We discovered our longings and understanding of the journey to God were similar. She thanked God many times for this, for someone who understood what she was saying and writing.

Barbara's writings have meant much to me personally and to my directees. Her practical and sometimes humorous remarks have been a real guide to both lay and religious to whom I have given them. Barbara speaks directly out of her own human experience, catching up the reader in the incidents and down-to-earth explanations she excels at. It is this quality of her work that unlocks the mysteries of the dark night of the soul to readers unfamiliar with it. One woman told me, "Only now, after reading what Barbara Dent wrote, do I begin to have an understanding of what St. John of the Cross and St. Teresa of Avila had to say. Barbara made it easy for me to come to grips with what was going on in my life." All the people I have directed to Barbara's writings have been helped, and they clamor for more.

Personally, I see Barbara's life and work as a vocation. She has received a special call to walk the route of the dark night and has been missioned to share her spiritual adventures with others through her writing. The finesse and expertise with which she writes help others see the hand of God in their own journey in the dark night. She has been a source of consolation and strength for everyone that I know who is perplexed by his own experience. Her vocation is unique in that she was married, is a mother of three and grandmother of ten, and is a Carmelite hermit. She brings all of these aspects to bear on her own understanding of the way of life that she explores in her writings and passes this knowledge along to others.

Barbara and I have a deep spiritual relationship in our Savior, Jesus Christ, and I see this as a pure gift from God who loves and cares for us in a gentle, tender, and loving manner, yet without compromise. We are either totally surrendered or we are not!

Fr. Bob Mitchell, OFM
Saskatchewan, Canada

The Marriage of
All and Nothing:

Selected Writings of
Barbara Dent

A Brown Habit

That long brown habit
hanging on the door recalls to me
a solid human body, tall and straight,
reliable and steady as Gibraltar, the guard
of that ancient sea and all its craft.

I touch it with my reverent hands
I rest my cheek against it. I feel at home
and safe at last, within our mutual
Beloved's arms; He holds me lest I fall.
He has my head against his heart.
His left hand clasps it close, his right hand
"doth embrace me." Such indestructible
enclosure makes me laugh at threats
and turns my tears to precious stones
he links into a chaplet and puts upon my head.

The brown habit was your robe
when you said Mass for us within my home—
a blessing and a treasure past all reckoning
and it was you who brought it to me
across the heaving oceans and cold, autumn skies, and then
presented it as gift and grace
adornment for my poverty, crowning for my solitude,
proof of the Christed love between us.

Living My Personal Journey

I Had to Let God Come In

Cross and Crown (June 1959)

I am a convert. I discovered Christianity long before I discovered Catholicism and worked during these early years to give myself more and more fully to God. I read widely in my search for truth, and I struggled with my intractable nature in a wholehearted effort to subdue it, that the will of God might be accomplished in me.

It was not until I had my first talk with a priest and read the books he lent me that the light really burst in on me in a radiant, life-giving cascade that changed my whole life.

It is true that what sometimes seems a sudden conversion is only the outward flowering of the mysterious, hidden workings of grace that have been gathering together for a long time for this hour of testimony. Looking back, I can see how my search for truth, begun almost as soon as I could think for myself, had been leading me to this moment and this place, even when it seemed I was denying and abusing all that the Catholic Church stood for.

I can see how my intense ache to be "good," with me since childhood, and my tears, sorrow, and despair that I was not and never could be "good," were nothing but the unrecognized yearning for holiness, that hunger and thirst after righteousness that Christ taught was blessed because those who were tortured by it would surely be satisfied.

I can see how I had been seeking Christ without knowing it, through all the human loves that had helped me and failed me, through all my painfully ecstatic worship of and response to beauty, through all the idealizations of creatures and consequent disillusionments, through all the yearnings, conflicts, delights, experiences, and long, dark days and months of desolation that had made up my life.

Quite suddenly, for no apparent reason, everything fitted together and made sense. The confused ideas, truths, half-truths, convictions that filled my mind formed themselves into an ordered pattern to which, day by day, as I studied and thought and prayed, new wonders and beauties were added. Then I realized that if I buried myself in Catholic books all my life, I should never come to the end of the truths they contained, never stop being enlightened and amazed, never want for stimulation, interest, and satisfaction.

The vehement yearnings of a too sensitive, too responsive heart became all at once centered on the sacred humanity of Christ. True, there were still many battles and agonies to be endured, but there was no doubt that my heart had found its home. Here was the one supremely satisfying Lover who could never be outdone in devotion and ardor, who received all that one longed to give and responded with all that one yearned to receive. With him there was no end to loving, no betrayals, no refusals, no disillusionments. I had reached the source and end of all loving, for Christ is love.

More than this—this Love had taken on tangible form. He lived, a willing captive, in the tabernacle of every Catholic church. Incredible though it seemed, one could receive him daily into oneself, the very Bread of Life, the fountainhead of grace, the essence of love, the meaning of existence. My heart had found its home. It rested in the tabernacle. It fed daily on the Blessed Sacrament. It had discovered repose at last.

My soul, in searching, had stumbled on its very purpose. My soul discovered that its only destiny is God; its way, Christ; its means, holiness. The dream of holiness that had haunted me in disguised form all my life suddenly revealed itself in its heavenly fullness, filling me with love and longing.

The Most Important Thing in Life

When I was haltingly beginning to acknowledge both God and Christianity, I asked myself in the midst of my travail: "What is the most important thing in life?" The answer came without hesitation: "The kingdom of heaven within." I was startled. I should never have expected a reply like that. But when I look back over my life, I see that this is precisely true. The times when I felt most alive, most real, most complete, were those when I experienced that state of being I had called "the kingdom of heaven within." At these moments peace established itself in me.

Without being able to define anything, I had known I was one with God and through him one with all people. Without being able to understand the why and how of the chaos of the world or the chaos in my own heart, I had yet been sure that all things were ordered well and held safely in the hollow of God's hand. Without being able to explain how, I had been filled with a tranquil joy.

Without any doctrinal background, I knew the truth—that God was love, that I lived and moved and had my being in him, that in some obscure fashion he was working out his will in me, and I might trust him and be at peace.

Yes, this was the kingdom of heaven within, and this was the most important thing in life for me. The times when I had entered into this state of soul had been the times when something enormous had happened to me. On my faith in this reality I could build the whole structure of my existence.

"Seek ye first the kingdom of heaven, and the rest shall be added unto you."

This realization was one of the crucial happenings of my life. Now I had a focal point. I had a purpose for living—full of meaning for me because it was based on the reality of my own experience. I knew exactly what I wanted from life—I wanted to enter more and more frequently, more and more completely, into this state of being called the kingdom of heaven within. From a bewildering disorder, life became astonishingly simple.

I thought back carefully over the circumstances I was in when I attained this state. These were what I would seek to recapture and cultivate. Many of the items of everyday living were found useless for my purpose, and I put other things in their place. I still did not know why, how, when, or where. I simply relied blindly on an experiential truth to be the light in my darkness.

What I really did was entrust myself to God, and looking back, I can see now the unerring way along which he led me to my true destination once I put my hand in his. Now that he had brought me to the Church, everything was clear. This state called the kingdom of heaven within was the very presence of God in the soul who loved him. It was the Christ-life within. To enter into God in this way was to enter into something of the state that the blessed enjoy in heaven, to become submerged in Christ, to taste here and now the blisses of eternity.

This was the life of identification with Christ to which all Christians are called, and which the Church extols as its goal. As members of his mystical body, they were incorporated into him, sharing his divine life, and fed by his sanctifying grace. The more fully they merged themselves with him, the more completely they were the instruments of God's will, the nearer they approached the state of the saints. Self still existed, but only as Christ's vehicle for loving, working, and suffering, only as a husk inhabited by the fertile seed of the Holy Spirit.

At last I understood the life principle of my soul, the source of all my restless yearnings and mysterious, luminous peace over the years. Now it was clear—God had been calling me, as he calls each soul he sends into the world, to a share in his divine life, to identification with his Son, to sanctity.

I saw this clearly. It made sense out of everything. It pulled together all the disjointed elements of my interior life. It roused in me an intolerable longing—and a grief—for I knew I was not good, and it seemed certain I never could be.

Abandonment to God

By the mercy and grace of God I found how to ease my longing and assuage my sorrow. Books helped me, but one surpassed all the others, clarifying everything. This book was Jean-Pierre de Caussade's *Self-Abandonment to Divine Providence.*

Caussade's doctrine, not a new one, is as old as Christianity itself and as new as St. Thérèse's "Little Way"—but it is expressed in an original and compelling manner, steeped in the spiritual wisdom of one who has battled in the arena of one's own soul and been director in the battles of many others. It reduces the spiritual life to a most inspiring simplicity. All great teaching about holiness has this directness and simplicity, this applicability to everyday life, this sound common sense and insight into human nature. Consider Christ's parables. Consider St. Thérèse's commonplace examples of daily living snatched up by grace, occasions of union with God. Caussade's teaching has the same unassuming homeliness, the same adaptable universality. It is for the beginner and the advanced, the unlearned and the educated, the sinner and the saint. It is for anyone and everyone who genuinely longs for holiness and is prepared to pay the price demanded by God.

It is strange how unaware people can be of what holiness is. Even Catholics, in spite of all the instruction given them and the help offered, can remain remarkably indifferent to this dynamic fact. Content with mediocrity, vaguely aware that there is another kind of existence but quite uninterested in it, they keep to the bare minimum required to escape hell.

Others are scornful or envious of the fervor and joy of the convert—and yet there is nothing keeping them from similar graces except their own refusal to give themselves completely to God.

The Church exists to make saints. This is only another way of saying that the Church exists to save souls, or to establish the kingdom of heaven on earth, or to administer the sacraments, or to safeguard divine truth, or to profess Jesus Christ, or to manifest the will of God—for the saved are those whose certain destiny is heaven, and no soul can enter heaven until it has been purged of all self-love and self-will and exists only for God—that is to say, until it is sanctified.

Before I began to investigate Catholicism, I thought a saint was an old-fashioned kind of Christian, a species several hundred years extinct, characterized by morbid bodily mortifications and an unhealthy emotional attitude toward God—in short, a psychological monstrosity. I even heard a cradle Catholic once remark with distaste after reading about some saint who underwent such things: "Oh, I don't like that sort of thing! It gives me the shudders!"

Of course, numbers of people long for sanctity in a pious, cozy way, with sentimental holy pictures and "special devotions." Caussade's way is not for these. It is for those who are prepared to venture beyond the mediocre, who dare to open themselves to divine grace, who have the courage to submit to its terrible purgations.

That sounds as if the way of self-abandonment were one of startling sacrifices, mighty deeds, heroic feats, and exploits that reduce the world to dumbfounded admiration.

It is not.

It is a way of obscurity and quietness; of hidden faithfulness and small, humiliating sacrifices; of interior silence and interior solitude; of humble self-effacement and tireless effort to subjugate self-will to God's will. For God sends us, each second, precisely what is most needed for our sanctification. By lovingly accepting the present moment as his will, and abandoning one's own will, second by second, in favor of his, one achieves union with him—which is, very simply, holiness.

My Discovery of the Saints

God, out of his love and goodness, had given me my "way." The methodical application of Caussade's teaching sustained me through a long period of suffering and trial, God's will for me, as a result of my conversion. When I could not understand his purpose, I could at least abandon myself in blind faith to his action. In this way I found a peace, though without joy, that upheld me through a time that would otherwise have been intolerable.

And yet I had not received the last of his gifts, for next he led me to discover the saints themselves. I began to read those modern biographies in which the lives and souls of those chosen ones are bared honestly and penetratingly to show ordinary people how other ordinary people become extraordinary.

The new world that had been opened to me was populated with the most fascinating and lovable people I had ever met. The reading of each book meant a new friend. A real person with so many of the struggles, trials, temptations, and consolations that I myself experienced walked out of the pages to greet me. This was no imaginary encounter, for they and I were all members of the mystical body, all one in Christ, and they, from heaven, looked down compassionately on me, heard my prayers, prayed for me, and gave me their help.

The communion of saints became a reality to me. These people were alive. Though some of them practiced fantastic bodily mortifications that I felt no desire or courage to imitate, and others experienced the prayer of mystical union in its highest form, nevertheless, all had had to contend with the same inward enemies that I daily strove against.

The things they did to subjugate their self-will, to practice virtue in countless small and mortifying ways, were a guide and inspiration. It was as if they went ahead of me as I walked, stumbling and falling in my clumsy efforts to follow them. They would beckon encouragingly. "This is the way," they called. "Don't give up. We'll pray for you. We'll help you. Just keep putting one foot in front of the other. Don't worry if you fall. Get up and go on again. Whatever you do, keep going.... Keep going...." They were there. They were real. Each book that I read made me want to take a photograph of my saint, to tell others about my new friend, to share the treasure I had found. I wanted to write and talk about each one, as if to say, "Here he is—here's the man you've been looking for— flesh and blood, frailty and strength, human and yet possessed by God. Have a look at him—because he's just like you and me. The otherness you see in him is God—and God wants to give himself to you just as he has given himself to him. All you have to do is let God come in."

All I have to do is let God come in....

Autobiography

Lacrimae rerum…The tears in things…
A Latin tag left lying about
in memory's outer reaches, school days' message
to watch your step, or else…
                    but I already knew
the hazards, had stumbled and fallen hard
upon my luckless face, with consequent bruises
and a few deep cuts that would not heal, but festered.

And I was aware, as one with an inborn gift
of instant computation, where the tears in things
were to be located, in whom, and how they overflowed
in drowning torrents, even upon whole nations
—the Jews, for instance.
                    It was many years
before I understood how one Jew once
had been assigned a role so intimately connected
with this awkward presence of the tears in things,
and in his arcane way, had then transmuted them
into those living waters with power to heal
all obstinate wounds, my own included.

Now I have fought my turbulent and tortured way
into that reservoir, immersed myself,
and found a priceless pearl that looks just like a tear.

One bathed with me, sharing holy droplets,
passing to me as I to him their blessing
on fingertips that touched and healed
our eyes of tears and made them shine with love.
            And then he changed his mind and went away.
            Lacrimae rerum…the tears in things….

[Untitled]

How for his praise
to order my new ways?
I would be no more myself, but he
using my breath and blood and song
to his own end, my life long.

So do I say—Master, your way
in mystery and wonder has evolved
my safety, and my curse resolved.
Glory and honor and homage are your due.
After the refining fire I bow to you.

Twelve Dark Years:
Cosmic Dusters, Glaciers, and the Void

Desert Call (Summer 1989)

Jesus said to Nicodemus, and by extension to all of us who seek to understand his message of renewal and love, that we have to be "born from above." We come into this world through natural birth. We enter that other world of the life of grace through a spiritual birthing process initiated by the Spirit herself, who is the midwife.

She will give us "living water," and this alone can quench our longing for the transcendent and satisfy the hunger of our hearts for a love that will last forever. We open our hearts to receive these waters of new life, to give birth to our new, graced self, by following Jesus, living as he lived, dying with him, and being included in his resurrection. That is the pattern of his and our consummation in that eternal life that the living waters initiate us into.

Jesus told us that the food and drink he lived by was doing the will of the Father in perfect, loving self-surrender. We, his disciples, have to do likewise. He promised us all the help we need, but he also warned us we would suffer. Our reply to the program he offers has to be that of Thomas the Twin: "Let us go too [to Jerusalem], and die with him" (John 11:16).

We have to die on one level before we can undergo that spiritual rebirth on the divine level and so become the liberated children of God. "If a man serves me, he must follow me. Wherever I am, my servant will be there too" (John 12:26).

The method, time, and place of our rebirthing, our death and resurrection, is hidden in the mystery of the divine redemptive plan for the whole world, but we can be certain that following Jesus must include going up to the Jerusalem of interior despoilation, and there entering with him that aspect of his passion, crucifixion, and death that God has chosen for us.

Faith and hope will then be all we have left to cling to. The process is likely to take years, and it will certainly hurt.

For me, it lasted twelve years.

During this time I was outwardly occupied being the solo parent of three school-age daughters, earning my living as a teacher, struggling with physical ill-health, writing, and doing university study. I was also living under a private vow of chastity and celibacy and attending Mass daily.

It was lucky that I had some distractions of work and study in my life, plus the responsibility of three children, so I could become absorbed in them. I doubt if I could have survived the severe, continuous interior suffering without such preoccupations. There were none of those alleviations and spiritual respites and refreshments one is supposed to enjoy during the dark night. It was a hard slog all the way—a long, difficult, terrible birthing process that reminds me of the arrival of my first child. In labor for a night and a day, I had been pushing hard for so long that I had become physically exhausted and the contractions were lessening. The midwife called the doctor, who found my baby had the cord round her neck and so could not be born naturally. He delivered her with forceps.

Something similar, on the spiritual level, happened to me when, in the last year of the twelve, God sent me a priest who in a real sense acted as deliverer of the "reborn" me.

What I recall and describe in the present article, written nearly twenty years after this rebirth (which significantly took place on my fiftieth birthday) was an essential part of that long, difficult, complicated labor of the spirit.

"The soul must be first of all brought into emptiness and poverty of spirit and purged from all help, consolation, and natural apprehension with respect to all things, both above and below. In this way, being empty, it is able indeed to be poor in spirit and freed from the old man, in order to live new and blessed life that is attained by means of this night, and is the state of union with God" (*Dark Night* 2:9:4).

Various metaphors came to me at the time, and later that helped me externalize my state and give it some kind of meaning. Here they are in detail, together with some factual description of what "being brought into emptiness and poverty of spirit and purged from all help and consolation" meant to one pilgrim on her way to union with Jesus in his resurrection.

One image that kept recurring was that of a cosmic eraser rubbing me out—a familiar image for a schoolteacher used to standing before a blackboard. Sometimes God exchanged the eraser for a bristly scrubbing brush and scrubbed me out. "This is one of my experiments that has failed," he was saying. "I'll get rid of it and start again."

I was experiencing myself in every way, especially spiritually, as ordinary and mediocre. That was one reason God was so intent on rubbing me out. I wasn't worth leaving on the blackboard. No one could learn anything from someone so nondescript.

My distress over this process was mixed up with my tendency to feel inferior and to strive to rectify matters by proving myself superior by means of outstanding achievement and success. Whenever I felt a thoroughly humiliated failure, the same remedy was called for. It was not easy to face the fact that vainglory, egotism, and ambition marred so much of my effort to serve God to his honor and glory rather than mine and even seeped through my spiritual life. Reading a biography of Newman, I was comforted that, though so gifted, he succeeded in little that he attempted and was humiliated even when he was so obviously holy and Christed and suffered from lifelong, periodic depression as well. And how about St. Thérèse? When she died, some nuns wondered what could be said of her in her obituary—she had been so ordinary and obscure, a nonentity, in fact. John of the Cross himself was "rubbed out" over and over, persecuted, disgraced, removed from office, humiliated, and treated as an outcast.

And the great Teresa spent eighteen years in mediocrity caused by her compulsion to run to the parlor and be adulated and made much of by those who came there especially to enjoy her company.

But all these were so clearly humble under these trials, and I was so lacking in the virtue of humility. It hurt to face this fact.... And Jesus? When I looked at him under the crown of thorns, I was ashamed of myself for such unfaithfulness to my purpose to be one with him in the total self-offering of his passion and crucifixion, for my self-pity, gloom, cries of woe, self-dramatization, and plain grizzling.

I must accept in peace that in my interior life, there seemed nothing but the most pedestrian states and progress. I plodded on in acute boredom, unable to pray or love God or experience any uplift. Most of the time I did not even seem to be plodding but rather to be transfixed in static, low-grade misery. Nailed to my cross—cross? This seemed far too exalted an interpretation of such a lowly state.

Or else I was waiting—for what or whom I could not remember. I waited in hope that was unhope, faith that was unfaith, love that was unlove. I waited in a heavy, night-bound fog of emptiness that penetrated to my depths, almost choking me. I starved for divine love, longed for human love, and felt I was denied both. God seemed to be jeering at me—as brutal soldiers did at helpless prisoners confined like animals in cages, or Jews in cattle trucks, or slaves roped together.

Or as onlookers did at Jesus as he hung on the cross.

I was a prisoner so ordinary and outcast, so without any powerful connections, so stripped of all indications of prestige or importance, that there was no chance of some influential person gaining me a reprieve and consequent release from my plight. I was a nobody, a no-thing, my name rubbed off the records. And I squirmed in my state.

✶ Everything humiliated me. It was nonsensical, but even my successes somehow registered as humiliations, while the genuine humiliations were devastating. The humiliation went on inside me irrespective of outward circumstances, though the Cosmic Duster Operator made sure that I no sooner thought someone was going to recognize how extraordinary I was, then he quickly erased either my "success" or "gift" or whatever it was that was impressing the person favorably and blotted out my natural enjoyment at the praise come my way. It was as if he kept reiterating, "You are nothing. I am ALL. Until you learn this lesson thoroughly, the treatment will continue. You have to realize that you've scarcely begun to understand and accept the rudiments of what is necessary in one who serves me. So—take that! And that! And that!"

God appeared to be acting as my sworn enemy (though I knew and constantly affirmed in faith that he remained my lovingly merciful heavenly Father). In my habitual way, I reacted by identifying myself as far as I could with Jesus in his passion. He was never my enemy, but always my brother, fellow sufferer, and intimate companion who knew and understood everything about the rubbing out process and humiliation.

✶ As well, I was afflicted with an almost constant sense of confusion and indecision. Even while my mind operated with clarity, vigor, and inspiration regarding classroom activities and university studies, leaping from insight to insight in an exhilarating way, mental confusion persistently invaded everything to do with my spiritual life and deciding what was God's will for me.

✳ There was the inability to make up my mind about my vocation, what was the best way to plan the rest of my life, where I should live once the last of my daughters left home for tertiary study or work, how I should earn my living—and the rest. No sooner did one course of action open up in apparent indication of what was God's probable will for me, then something happened to destroy certainty and thwart my efforts to comply. Bewilderment resulted. I never ceased to seek his will as my priority—but I found him remarkably cagey at revealing with any clarity what it was!

✳ Time and again I felt he expected me to stop short as I galloped in one direction, heading where I believed he was pointing, and in one swerve turn and gallop in the opposite direction without pause or question. With his scrubbing brush he had already erased all signposts, smeared all maps so they could not be accurately read except in disjointed sections, and even caused landslides to block the very road he had told me to travel. Often I was so confused about what he wanted that I felt the urge to give up.

✳ To give up aiming at wholehearted love of him and be as "ordinary and mediocre" as he was showing me I was. To give up clinging to his will, and follow my own natural longings. To give up all this renunciation, and instead enjoy life in the way most "normal" people did. To give up my strict daily regimen of Mass, Office, trying to pray, self-discipline and self-denial, and have a last fling. To renounce my vows and set out to locate a husband to share life and love with. To stop suffering and somehow find an easygoing happiness.

"To stop suffering...?"

I did not know how. And anyway, I knew if I tried to escape from all this rubbing out by giving up my Catholic life and ideals, I would not find happiness, but even worse disaster. I would destroy myself and anyone else I became involved with. Under all the confusion, my dedication remained staunchly unshakable. The problem was that only seldom was I given a brief awareness of this fact in the midst of the confusion.

I said to God, "I believe—whatever you do with me and with my life." But mostly my affirmations had no more meaning to me in the discordant babble and muddle of my so-called (which I felt nonexistent) spiritual life, than the mouthings and gestures of an idiot.

I was quite likely to hurl at God a savage challenge like, "You want me to do your will, don't you? Then why do you refuse to show me what it is?" There were times when I was enraged against him and his ways. It only seemed to provoke celestial laughter.

Worry, anxiety, and uncertainty eradicate peace of mind and the ability to float easily in endless love.

I had always feared delusion and understood how it could wreck one's relationship with God. To counter any possibility of it, I had all along done everything I could to reveal honestly and fully to my directors my interior state and outward actions. Yet, even though I was reassured over and over, the doubts about myself and my spiritual life and prayer (nonprayer) recurred. I suppose it was a kind of scrupulosity.

Rereading St. Teresa, I found that she too constantly sought reassurance, through a series of directors and advisors, some good and some bad, that she was not deluded. She too suffered anguish when it was implied that she might be, and tremendous relief when she was affirmed and encouraged.

All I could do in my numb, dumb spiritual state—so foreign to hers, but not too unlike Thérèse's and Jane Frances's—was keep on telling my director the same things that persisted in worrying me, including the fear of having succumbed to lukewarmness. When he comforted and reassured me once again, I would experience a brief peace of mind, only to have the same cycle monotonously repeat itself later on.

My constant remedy was to do my best to make acts of self-abandonment over everything, telling myself and God that I believed he knew what he was doing, and I accepted his will under all its disguises. I was mediocre, in performance, but I did keep on trying, and I concluded that God kept on muddling up my life precisely so I would persevere in trying to abandon myself. He wanted me to float in idiotic trust that he did all things well—an acrobatic feat that I was rather clumsy at.

Part Two

I constantly had to endure a sense of basic absurdity in my life. Because of this, I found stimulation and analogies in my readings in existentialism in connection with some of my literature papers. Meaning, in the ultimate sense, in a way recognizable to human intellect and logic, seemed to have been erased from my life.

"As flies to wanton boys, are we to the gods. They kill us for their sport." There was no logic in God's dealings with me, or with my loved ones, or with the world at large. Useless, demeaning suffering afflicted so much of humanity, and there was so little one could do to ease it. The *lacrimae rerum* inundated the universe. Faustus, in Marlowe's play, cried out, "See, see, where Christ's blood streams in the firmament!" and pleaded for but one drop of it to save him from despair and hell. The cry recurred over and over in my mind. It was the only answer I could find for "the tears in things." Yet this very answer was in itself shot through and through with absurdities.

I had for many years possessed a black and white drawing of Christ on the cross. Like the Dali image, both were floating in midair, only this cross was horizontal, not vertical. Across it and the crucified Lord flooded waves of what might be clouds, or the tears of humanity, or Christ's own blood.

The powerful representation of grief immersing the Savior in what was also a redeeming flood of grace flowing from himself had intense meaning for me. It recalled Faustus's despairing cry. It reaffirmed the reality of the link between suffering and salvation. It even gave me a vague hope that Jesus did include my sufferings in that saving torrent, and so expunged the absurdity from my life.

My director's affirmations of the positive aspect of my plight temporarily gave me the comfort of meaning, but soon the cosmic duster rubbed it out again, leaving only a nonsensical scribble that gave the opposite of comfort.

So often my only possible prayer was, "Lord, I believe. Help thou my unbelief." To make such a faith statement in such circumstances was to claim floating even while grounded—an absurdity, a paradox. But was not faith itself absurd? Could faith exist unless constantly challenged by absurdity?

Connected with the drawing of Christ was my own sense of floating impotently in a void. At times the lack of support, the emptiness, the absence of God, was terrifying. It reminded me of the film *2001: A Space Odyssey* when the astronaut's connecting life cord with the mothership was severed by the computer, Hal, which had apparently gone mad. The image of this human being in a space suit, trailing his umbilical cord and condemned to drift forever in the infinite void of space had horrifying impact on me. (It was to recur even more cogently some eighteen years later.)

This was how I experienced myself—like some kind of rejected waste material, cast off and obliterated by an apparently insane God of absurdity into the void of the not-God, a nowhere, a nothingness, an eternal lostness.

It was the sense of being damned, while continuing to affirm in bare faith that I was saved by a God who was neither insane nor absurd, but perfect wisdom, love, and tender enfoldment.

Abysmal loneliness was inseparable from the void experience. It was characteristic for me to feel (and be) alone, not fitting in or belonging anywhere. A sense of alienation often possessed me, coupled with that of worthlessness and rejection by God and humans. This was no doubt linked with my psychological state, but it went much further than that. Again, grace was perfecting nature, and God was using what was already there as a means of spiritual purification.

Though efficient in my work, caring and careful as a mother, outwardly cheerful, free with jokes and quips, animated in conversation, interested in others, responsible in my behavior toward them and a ready listener—inwardly I often felt cut off from them all, even my own daughters. This would not have mattered much if I had not so strongly felt separated from God also.

It was a loneliness, an experience of being essentially alone, somewhere at the very core of my being where I should have been sure that "underneath are the everlasting arms" that would not "let a hair of my head be harmed." God had rubbed out his arms, and indeed his whole presence, leaving nothing but an infinite blank. He had become the apophatic entity who had no name, who "may be well loved, but not thought."

He was beyond all attributes, existing in, and himself being, the Infinite Void. He was uncompromisingly enigmatic in his ways and purposes (except that they were always providential, though not in a way that human understanding could penetrate). Consequently, he could be approached only by naked faith, for "clouds and darkness" perpetually concealed his "face"—which, anyway, humans cannot see and live. (The case of Moses is ambiguous!) And yet...and yet....

I knew, had directly experienced, had existed in the truth of the fact that this All-and-Nothing (no-thing) enclosed me. In him I had known with certainty that "I lived and moved and had my being."

How, then, was it possible for me to be permeated by such loneliness? Hidden in my heart, I knew the answer—though it gave me no comfort. It was because it was his will, and my own through my redemptive offerings so plainly and repeatedly expressed in the past, for me to hang on the cross with Jesus in a state of negative floating and to join him in his cry of dereliction in this vertiginous blank. "My sacrifice, O God, is a broken and contrite heart" (Ps. 51).

One image that constantly recurred to me during these years was that of a glacier's slow, inexorable grinding away of all protuberances from the walls and floor of the valley it majestically flowed down. I was that valley; the glacier was God's action in my life. It was grinding to dust (in an intensified version of rubbing or scrubbing out) all the protuberances of my self-love and self-will impeding its purposes.

When a glacier recedes, it reveals its valley as U-shaped. The smoothness of the rock is remarkable. The grinding process has taken centuries in its unhurried but efficient method of producing the desired result.

Now, at the time of compiling this record, I see that, in a similar way, God's grace (often registering on me as a curse because of what appeared to me at the time to be its destructive effects) was grinding away from my clinging heart all attachments and desires contrary to his purpose. Worldly and even "holy ambitions," as my director called them, had to go.

So did longings for human love, marriage, fulfillment. All romanticizings, idealizings, and illusions, as well as delusions, had to go. All tethering ropes, all cherished concepts of a human origin (like my own ideas of what spiritual love and holy tenderness were like), all longings to be "mothered and fathered," all cosseting of my inward child, all my own ideas of what God's time and way for me should be, had to be jettisoned.

Using various metaphors, Jesus had constantly reiterated that his followers were not to set their hearts on any kind of "treasure" at all on this earth. Our treasure is to be in him and the kingdom of heaven within. For his sake and his work, we are to sever every human relationship, even the closest family ties, that threaten to come between him and us.

✳ "Anyone who prefers father or mother, son or daughter, to me is not worthy of me" (Matt. 10:35). He was inexorable about it.

The glacier-grinding was the most penetrating of all the erasures, and the most pitiless. It reduced me to destitution. I moved beyond the ordinariness of mediocrity, and even poverty, into beggary and complete despoliation.

When he asked me, "What have you that you have not received?" God intended me to be able to answer honestly from a broken and contrite heart, "Nothing, Lord. Nothing at all." He rubbed out the light of awareness of his loving Presence and left only "darkness absolute." I caught myself often thinking Milton's "dark, dark, dark, irremediably dark, amid the blaze of noon."

Light was consolation; surety; confidence; fulfillment in mutual love; hope that could conceive of an end worth hoping for; joy in the heart-to-heart encounter with a risen, triumphant Lord; daylight and sunlight in his radiant Presence. It was journey's end, God saying, "Well done, my good and faithful servant. Come and share the joy of your Lord." In "darkness absolute" I was sunk deep in the Stygian inner abyss where daylight never penetrated. "Out of the depths have I cried to thee"—only most of the time I felt my mouth closed by the impact of his own fist, and I was dumb in misery.

"I was speechless and opened not my mouth, because it was your doing. Take away your scourge from me. At the blow of your hand I wasted away. With rebukes for guilt you chasten me; you dissolve like a cobweb all that is dear to me" (Ps. 38).

This was desolation, doubt, and loss of confidence in both self and God; absence of both fulfillment and love; hope reduced to nothing but a hidden kernel in the core of despair; misery consuming a heart crucified in the pierced Sacred Heart of the

Lord's dead, entombed body; God saying, "Out of my sight, you wicked and unfaithful servant, and be lost in everlasting night" (see Matthew 25).

When light is rubbed out, the danger is of succumbing to a permanent state of unalleviated melancholy. Only stubborn affirmations of faith and faulty but persistent efforts at self-abandonment to divine providence saved me from this. In some obscure, nameless way, grace (which enabled me to cling to God somehow, somewhere) blessed my misery, turning it into negative floating and making it spiritually fruitful for myself and others, though at the time I was scarcely ever able to believe this, except briefly, when my director once more reassured me.

Isaiah reminded me to tell myself, "It is the Lord who speaks.... I, the fashioner of darkness, the creator of light; I, the maker of peace, the author of calamity—I, the Lord, am the doer of all this" (Isa. 21:11—Knox).

If God was in control, what was there to fear? Even if he went on rubbing, scrubbing, scouring, and grinding till there was nothing left of me but a sliver of adamant will that would not give up loving and trusting him—what did it matter?

However I felt, whatever images of disaster and destruction haunted me, the fact was that in that faithful, graced sliver of will, I knew I was safe in his arms forever and not a hair of my metaphorical head would be harmed.

What was lacking was only the comfort and reassurance one would expect to derive from such convictions. Only the trimmings were absent. I was safe in the rest.

Dom Vital Lehodey was the author of *Holy Abandonment,* a book to which I frequently referred during these years of dark trial. In a biography about him, I read how he constantly suffered from severe nervous depression, which was aggravated when he was fatigued or under emotional strain. He would go away alone while he struggled to practice perfect abandonment under God's action, no matter how he was feeling. He would even shut himself away for several days on end. Yet at this time he was far advanced in holiness and prayer and had already written his book on abandonment. He admitted that, because of his sensitive temperament and recurring attacks of melancholy, he had great need of consolation. His book was based on his own personal experiences during twenty years of desolation. It was his reassurance to himself, and to others in like distress, during the torture of uncertainty, inability to feel joy in God or religion, and severe trials and temptations concerning faith, hope, and love. So he too "whistled in the dark" of his soul's night. I felt I had met a staunch and understanding friend and fellow traveler.

Despite all disturbances, I knew my own prayer was an almost wordless and continual act of loving abandonment that went on under everything all the time. It was always dry and painful, and when I was racked by the need for affection and understanding or by depression, it became a cry of anguish. Yet, automatically, somewhere deep below it all, I went on saying "yes." Down there in the depths my soul, I was making a continual act of abasement and worship. I was the twenty-fifth elder throwing down my crown and prostrating myself before the grandeur and might of God. I was Peter's sister casting myself at Christ's feet and crying, "Have mercy on me, O Lord, for I am a sinful woman," and being, somewhere beyond feeling, absolutely certain of that tender mercy and love.

God came to me only in the darkness and the void. Strange how he could seem a void when, in faith, I was certain he was omnipresent.

When I deliberately set myself to "mental prayer" in a specific time set aside for praying, I was assailed with such a strong sense of impotence and barren aridity that it was all I could do to control the impulse to run away. Restlessness and boredom tormented me.

I could think of nothing to say to God except an automatic, "My God, I love you," and "give me yourself." These entirely lacked unction and were as if meaningless. They were like dry sticks rattling together in a breeze.

When I tried to force my intellect to frame "meaningful" prayers, several things could happen. Either I lost the thread after a few words and was drowned in distractions again, or else I started to make up a nice little thing like one of my articles and after a while observed what I was doing and said with pleasure and self-congratulation, "Ah! I'm praying properly!" even while I knew it was not real prayer at all, but an intellectual exercise. I longed to be able to be still, leaving my intellect quite alone, while all I did was stay closer to God than breath.

I felt that my real prayer was simply doing nothing. Usually it was so intensely boring that I could not keep it up for long. I was sure the prayer and self-offering were indeed there, but so deep down inside me that nothing reached either my mind or my emotions, and so the restlessness and boredom invaded me.

The nearest I came to any kind of repose or satisfaction in prayer was on rare occasions before the tabernacle when an artesian well of "Oh God...Oh God...Lord...Lord..." broke the surface of its own accord. It would flow on and on monotonously. It calmed me so that a kind of stillness would descend—or well up—and I would become aware that I was resting in God, as in a temporary safehouse. It was as if I were prostrated before the altar as the priests are on Good Friday, not daring to look God in the face, yet compelled always to stay near him in this position of adoration and abandonment that was intimately part of the Passion of the Lord. I was impotent to pray except in such ways.

I comforted myself with the thought that surely it was the spirit that communed with God, for all the rest would dissolve with death. So it must be possible for any spirit to be praying, while the rest (intellect, memory, emotions, even heart) remained unabsorbed in and unaffected by the prayer—except when later the prayer was put into practice by serving God as his will dictated, and refusing to give up, no matter what. "Yea, though he slay me, yet will I cling to him."

Alone

When I'm alone in the dark
and you have left me—although I know
You never do that, but knowledge is one thing
and feeling another—it is then that no comfort
comes from anywhere or anyone. I call—
you do not answer. Since it is a soundless wail
I must not wonder if a soundless answer
comes my way, but is not acknowledged or heard.

I am so far down the ladder of faith I do not register
(except on special occasions when you pander to me)
with my clamoring ears such whispers of assurance
that never reach my heart. Have pity, Lord.
Have mercy on me, a sinner, who yearns for festive meals
when all you offer me is paupers' leftovers!
I do my best to value what you hand me
to quell my longings and my avid hungers
to bow in humility before your will for me
and accept with gracious willingness
your starvation diet in trusting meekness
and awareness of the truth.

Alas, my score is nil. The loneliness is absolute.
I know your love is here—but do not feel its comfort.

Is this purgatory? Or have I strayed into hell?

Ways—Lost and Found

I've lost my way—and yet I haven't.
How could I, when he stated categorically, "I
am the Way, the Truth, and the Life"?
He is undoubtedly my maze-like Way.
I cannot lose him, for he is the tangled route
I take to get from here to there. He is
the one companion who never leaves my side.
Sometimes he uses fanciful disguises—
like a cloud of mist enveloping him and me—
soft and clinging, moist and indefinable,
assuming shapes that challenge imagination
so that I tell myself in irritation, "That's not him.
Where's he gone now? Who does he think he is?
Why does he taunt and tease? Surely
I have enough to put up with and do not need
phantasms hanging round my morning muesli?"

He laughs. He likes a joke, whether its origin
is in him or me. His laugh is male and hearty
yet never cruel or unseemly. With him
everything is in proportion, directed to
its rightful end, rounding off each event
with a little flourish of rightful comment.

Frozen Desert

This is not the place of quagmires and quicksands
it is the dry, arid, frozen desert. No animals
graze here. Not even rabbits come. All is still
save for the inane chatter of myriads of varied insects.
Alone, I wander here under the sun. But its heat
is tempered to my age and weakened legs. The aridity is eased
occasionally by an unexpected spring (that soon dries up!)
I plod along, all inspiration shrivelled by the drought.

Then come the tongues of fire setting rubbish piles alight—
but, in limbo, light is soon quenched by boredom.
The Shepherd has gone to someone much more needy
and I bless his compassionate feet and hands, his words
that bring such comfort, ease and peace, his face alight with love,
his living presence glowing with muted splendor,
gentle to those failing eyes
and I pray these blessings come to me when he remembers
        to return.

Desert Home

You are the desert.
        Oh, what sunsets
burnished like polished brass!
Sunrises in skies as clear as arctic lakes!
And you yourself striding beside the sun!
You soar on eagle's wings and hover
where those dried-out watercourses wait
to explode in flowers after brief
but drenching rains you trail behind you
as you glide and jubilate aloft.

You are the desert.
        These flowers both emerge
and drink from your pulsating arteries.
Their loveliness reflects your face, sunset
and sunrise throb with your blood's eternal life
centering itself in you—then bursts,
like firework displays, upon this desiccated world.

Wherever your jewelled feet speed
over barren hill and dehydrated hollow there bursts
the glory and the grace of leaping freshet, unfurling bud.

You are the desert.
        I meet you here.
This is our trysting place.
Face to face we gaze where you reveal
wonders I never guessed at.
From these gasping cavities you make

a habitation of such rich delights
that I can only kiss your hands
and kneel before your flower-garlanded feet.

This desert is my chosen, everlasting home.

Triumph of the Cross:
Presence and Interpenetration

Desert Call (Spring 1989)

It was Tuesday.

Some days I was well enough to dress and go to Mass—other days, I was not. This was one of the "was not" days. Fr. Christopher had brought me Communion at 7 A.M. After that I had my breakfast on a tray in bed and then began reading the morning paper in an entirely normal way.

In the light of what began to happen, I think it of particular significance that I had so recently and formally renewed my unreserved gift of the whole self to God for him to use in whatever ways he chose, irrespective of the cost to me. I had always left the results in peace entirely to him. I knew he would use me one way or another, but that was his business. I never went about expecting or anticipating being used or to suffering something spectacular.

What had been recently in my heart and mind were joyful, peaceful, grateful prayers to do with the fulfillment of spiritual love and holy tenderness. However, on this morning of my fiftieth birthday, I was aware of a familiar substratum of muted misery. I was so used to this that it was almost on par with my heartbeats and breathing. It was not depressing me or commanding my attention; I felt "normal," if very tired, and my mind was occupied with what

I was reading in the newspaper when what I can only think of as "an invasion" began to assert itself.

About 9:30 A.M. the underground misery surfaced properly into consciousness and gradually intensified. This was my individual kind of suffering that I regularly offered Jesus for his redemptive work, the kind that also at times peaked to a crazy violence that made me fear madness and diabolic activity and that directors had considered salvific.

On this birthday morning the personal suffering did not reach that pitch. Instead, it began to expand into something rather different or perhaps only additional.

First it enveloped my mother's suffering, both when she had lived just down the street and at the present when she lay almost senile in the rest home bed far away. Her misery seemed to take possession of me, so that we fused together to become a single afflicted being. This was not an imaginative sympathy or empathy, but an existential blending. *of or relating to existence, based on exp.*

It became so insistent and intense that I could not concentrate any longer on reading the paper or on anything else—I could attend only to it. There was no evading or quenching its presence.

As I lay there, helplessly passive, it penetrated further to become the suffering of others, friends, acquaintances, people I had only heard of but empathized with and felt compassion for. The cumulative effect of this was already so severe that I felt like screaming with pain, but did not. Worse was to come. Near noon I received an even profounder stab, calculated to annihilate all defenses between me and other human beings. It pierced my heart in an awful spasm as "the world's agony"—which is the name I have always given to this day's experience.

It was a bit like the birthing process when the head of the fetus is about to present itself, and the mother feels her body is going to

To destroy completely, to reduce to nonexistence, defeat, vanquish

be burst apart, as if it cannot dilate further—and yet it does, so her child can come to be.

Or as when one is in a race and the finishing line is quite close, only one's lungs and heart are ready to burst with the tiniest further effort. Yet to make it will get one there in time to benefit others, and so from somewhere comes the will and strength for one extra spurt—and one is past the mark.

Only for me there was no sense of achievement, but only spasm after spasm of anguish, as my effort intensified to remain open to receive what God was letting happen to me. I had no alternative, though I suppose I could have screamed, "No! No more! Stop now!" only it never occurred to me to do this. Indeed, it was impossible for me to withdraw my inner self from where it was. All I could do was passively let the ordeal happen till God chose to stop whatever it was.

The sense of a Power beyond myself at work in and through me was overwhelming.

I kept making up my mind that I must get up and dress, go out of the house, ring a neighbor, find something—anything—to do, as long as it distracted me and eased the suffering. But, strangely, every time I made an effort to rise, I not only felt too physically exhausted to stand up and move about but the invasion intensified to such a degree that it made me weep helplessly. As long as I stayed passive and still in my bed, I could bear it. But if I tried to make myself do anything that required effort or concentration, I was risking total collapse or madness. R. was away on holiday. I was alone in the house. There was no prospect of anyone coming, nor could anyone have understood or helped me.

It must have been awhile after noon when the next degree of identification occurred and I was immersed consciously in Christ's "continuous passion," which I had so long ago agreed to share with him in my own heart and life. I can only describe it as such a concentrated awareness of Jesus suffering in me that it obliterated any possibility of attending to anything else. I reached the stage where I knew I could not bear it any longer, so, distraught and beside myself at the power of his passion happening within me, I forced myself to get up. I put on my dressing gown and went shakily to the kitchen, determined to try to dispel all this insubstantial world of woe by something as mundane as eating. But I got no further than the table. I had to sit down or I would have fallen. There was no chance of concentrating on anything but what was going on within me.

The climax must have come some time before 3 P.M. It was as if an enormous tsunami crested and broke upon me. But also upon Christ and humanity incorporated into me—and I into them. The immense, inconsolable grief of all humanity enclosed in his passion had burst out to engulf my own heart and soul.

Under its impact I collapsed to lie helplessly on my face on the floor. I was Jesus in Gethsemane pleading for the cup to go away, yet knowing I would drink it—was drinking it—had drunk it over and over since 1955.

I was Jesus fallen under the cross as he toiled up Calvary and I was crushed under its weight—which was not only wood, but the sins and the woe of all the afflicted world.

And I was Jesus nailed on the cross, enduring the awareness of being abandoned by his one rock and refuge, the Father, as he "became sin" for the sake of those who were crucifying him. I was stripped of every consolation, support, and love. I was alone in the bottomless loneliness of the damned—only Jesus was there too, for "he descended into hell."

And I was also myself—this weak and foolish Barbara, stricken and helpless and on the verge of madness.

At this time of writing, it is just about twenty years since the above happening, yet the terrifying reality of it remains clear in my mind—a unique and, I hope and pray, unrepeatable event for me. On it my life was broken into two parts—the before and the after. It brought about a fundamental change in my inner being.

I suppose the climax lasted only about a quarter of an hour or so, but it seemed an age or to be outside time. As it faded, it left me almost as if life itself had drained out of me, but, thank God, it took the anguish with it.

Though shaky and weak, I was now in my right mind and calm. I ate something and then dressed, determined to get out of the house and away from the scene of my "birthday treat." I drove slowly and carefully to church, and after sitting praying for some time, was closeted in the confessional. When I told Fr. Christopher as coherently and unadornedly as I could exactly what had happened, I sensed it made him afraid, yet he comforted and confirmed me, assuring me of the huge benefit to others this happening had been.

I knew that "the strength of Christ" that he had the previous day conferred on me like a sacrament under the influence of the Spirit had been given so I would be able to endure "the world's agony." He had been the intermediary for the most complete union with Christ I had ever been granted. Our own loving union in the Lord had passed on to me, through our spiritual interpenetration, the graces, and power of his priestliness. Perhaps it had even made me a kind of priest according to "the priesthood of the faithful" with Christ the eternal high priest, with power "to intercede for others" while prostrate on my own dining-room floor under the tsunami of humanity's woe.

I knew that, though fully conscious, I had been rapt out of myself in a way I had never conceived possible. It seemed I had been given the grace to receive and endure an ecstasy of agony.

The psalmist says, "Hear now, all you who fear God, while I declare what He has done for me" (Ps. 65).

If my "declaration" is couched in terms of "mystical marriage," it is because the Song of Songs made an indelible impression on me at the age of sixteen, as did readings of John of the Cross and Teresa during my first year in the Church, coupled with my own prayer experiences at the time. Marriage symbolism in all its poetic richness was the only type that came anywhere near adequately expressing what spiritual copenetration, presence, intermingling, fusion, invasion—and the rest—meant to me experientially.

✳ Mystical marriage begins at baptism, for it is then that Christ is first infused into the soul. I was lucky to have had adult con-version and baptism, and that it succeeded the deep realization of what this meant theologically and actually, coupled with a well-developed, intense longing for Christ, a willingness to share his passion with him and a proven faith that the sacrament would truly make me one with him.

✳ After "the world's agony," the change in my interior life was immediate and dramatic, though for a few days I was too exhausted to register much, except that the ancient, twelve-year-long, apparently incurable suffering arising from spiritual darkness and desolation had completely gone. In its place was a growing ex-periential awareness of Christ the Beloved's tender presence that was similar to what I had had in my early days in the Church, except that now it was immeasurably deeper, surer, quieter, and more ethereal.

It was as if I had moved into another dimension of being. There was light everywhere—increasing as the days passed and the shock of the world's agony diminished. All my life the sun had been a powerful symbol of God for me, and now it became so for the Risen Lord. Like the sun, he was abroad and shedding his trans-figuring glory within and outside me. He was everywhere in wedding regalia, and rejoicing and alleluias accompanied him. I do not mean I saw him with my bodily eyes or with the eyes of the imagination. He was just "there"—a presence, a reality—but not to be seen or touched or apprehended by any of the senses. And he had risen from the tomb as Victor and universal Savior, bearing in his side, hands, and feet those wounds that were also glorified, grace streaming from them into me and the whole world.

All this registered accurately and convincingly somewhere deep within me in some spiritual place that is unlocatable, for it has no concrete dimensions.

It was spring, and the entrancing symbolism of new growth, the revitalization of plant and tree and bird life after the winter, was part of my release into a fructifying, healing, spiritual embrace. I felt impregnated by Christ with Christ.

I floated in Light; I floated in Love.

Not only that, but they permeated me, till I felt drenched in the divine Presence, penetrated by it to my depths. The prayer of presence and penetration came to me and stayed with me, but in a much more ethereal and inward way than all those years earlier after my baptism.

It was like the arrival of a weary, travel-marred pilgrim in the promised city of delight and rest—like the last chapters of Revelation with their imagery of heavenly homecoming: a new heaven and a new earth (and a new Barbara); the bridal celebration; water from the well of life given freely; victory gained at last after awful warning; the resplendent glory of God; the city of incomparable beauty; no need for sun and moon, for the radiance of God filled the whole place; no need for temple, for the crucified and risen Lord was its temple and its light; no night ever again; no weeping and tears and mourning ever again; the living waters, crystal clear, flowing everywhere to give life, to revive and invigorate; God's own name in my forehead; robes washed clean; the ever and everness of it all.

To have the water of life, and have it free.

The imagery of the living waters flowing abundantly into, for, and through me, was insistent. I knew I was at last what I had craved to be—a channel for Christ's redemptive love and peace for others. He was using me, as I had pleaded to be used, but now it was not in the nightbound mode of interior suffering and desolation, but in the glory, joy, love, light, and tenderest healing of all wounds. The inner, essential loneliness that had afflicted me all my life, intensifying so heartbreakingly over the previous twelve years, had vanished. It was replaced by the loving enfoldment of Jesus' arms.

He was both everywhere about me and blissfully within me. It was as if I tasted him spiritually, and the taste was exquisitely sweet and fulfilling.

Though I was as arid as ever, it was a different brand of aridity. Whereas before, all had been only painful darkness and obliterating fog, now the sun shone all the time behind a silvery, beautiful, luminous mist. I was in a state of permeating, gentle peace and blessedness, so that I prayed the Divine Praises over and over. "Blessed be God...Blessed be His Holy Name...." He was no longer my enemy. On the contrary, I had that profound, certain, constant sense of his mercy, goodness, and loving-kindness. I was sure that Christ had claimed me finally for his own in a deeper, more permanent, and indelible way than ever before.

It was all very sensitive, gentle, and interior. It was so delicate that a lot of the time I scarcely knew that it was happening. But then the peace that passes all understanding would well up in a wordless, quiet prayer of thanksgiving and fulfillment.

One significant, ruling pattern of my life had at last reached completion in Christ, and I had been released from its compelling power over me to arouse the four passions of joy, hope, fear, and grief to an ungovernable degree. The rejection syndrome had ceased to dominate me, quelled, if not finally obliterated by divine love and comfort. At last my inner house was at rest, and the profound peace and quiet in my material house where I now spent hour after hour of my days, day after day, alone and in communion with God, resting and recuperating quietly in my Beloved, was symbolic of my interior state. All the time I was aware of resting, floating, and abiding in the Trinity.

The great, fathomless, painful void scoured out in the dark by the grinding glacier had at last stopped aching and crying out, for it was being filled with him it longed for. My state was one of being intravenously fed. No satisfaction to the appetites or senses, but something indefinable that was yet indeed nutritious to my whole being. I felt like a reservoir being silently and invisibly filled with the living waters.

This state of muted bliss, though it ebbed and flowed somewhat, lasted for several months. I was drowned in love and peace. They flowed up silently, but with immense force within me so that the words, "fountains of living water shall flow from his breast," kept coming back to me. I often "saw" a lotus thrusting up from dark, still waters to open to the light—pure, waven, exquisite, numinous.

It was not I who made the fountain play within me, but the Spirit who was "playing" at possessing me.

God permeated the whole universe, and this was evident to me as never before. Christ, through whom all things were made and held in being, was expressing himself in all beauty, displaying his loveliness, grace, power, virility in which my eyes and ears delighted in. Continuously he sent me messages, every one an affirmation of love, of his desire to pleasure me, of his possession of me, of his saying to me, "You are mine. I give you this beauty and this peace because I put my seal on you. I have claimed you, and now I will never leave you. I want you to look on me everywhere, to be immersed in me in all beauty. And I am in you, too. I have penetrated and permeated you with my own being. My will is to possess and fill you utterly with myself."

My constant affirmation was "I am my Beloved's and He is mine." Only the imagery of human love in the union of marriage could convey the nature of the spiritual actuality.

Whereas before I could believe I was "working" only when I was suffering, now I was certain I was "working," and powerfully too, simply by loving, by doing nothing but loving my Beloved and receiving his love. I knew without any doubt that this was enough. He put his own love into me, and this was the fountain of living waters that kept on playing in me without a sound, without movement. It was his love now active and working within me, in that place emptied out by the dissolving of the syndrome, the vacuum of longing at last filled with what it ached for. I no longer loved with my love, but with his.

Thus he was working powerfully through me for others in ways I did not know and had no need to know. My total concentration upon him, won after such long agony, was reparation for many, many loveless lives. By giving him a home to claim as his own, I localized him in time and place so that invisible powers of grace could flow out from him through me as his instrument for that work of redemption that he had become incarnate for and that he had chosen to include me in, pitiful and poor though I was.

Was not his strength made perfect in our weakness? And were not all things possible with him?

The hours I spent under the trees in the seclusion of my garden, so aware of beauty as an aspect of him, were dedicated to prayer, self-offering, and a communion too deep for words or emotion. Wonderingly I said to myself, "I am. And where I am, I am in him."

It was being experientially proved to me that these words were indeed true: "In him I live and move and have my being." He had sunk so deeply into me that we were interpermeated. How could he extricate himself ever again? Surely he would continue his work until every uttermost shred of my being was filled with him as my veins, arteries, and capillaries were with blood.

I also experienced myself as blended with all those who were dedicated to him in love, and who thus understood my love for him and united themselves with me in it. This communion was the deep and blessed mystery of reciprocal Christian love: "That they all may be one, as you and I, Father, are one."

My lifelong intuitions and longings about love were now being sealed as authentic, as truths that others and I were actually living. I was one with my beloveds in Christ. His peace washed through them. The blessedness of his presence was evident in them, in me, in us.

The pledge was fulfilled, the truth won, grace at last triumphant over all obstacles. The vision that had haunted me all my life was now a reality within me, and I was moving all the time even more deeply into it to possess it, for it to possess and transform me forever.

Overwhelmed, I bowed down before the Lord, praising and adoring him, rendering up my whole life and self to him to use as he chose.

In Praise of God's Two Hands

Your one hand cups me in your sheltering palm—
this insignificant insect that is I
lately emerged from metamorphosis, now quivering
in expectation.

    I agitate
my gauzy wings, alert for currents of warm air
to lift me high into the sun-drenched spaces.
I wait, antennae tremulous,
my tiny, vulnerable form
readied for flight.

    Instantaneous, out of this cloudless sky,
eclipse falls.
    Upon your concave palm
your other hand bears down. The two
clamp shut as tight as oyster shells.
I, trapped within, discover night.

Stifled, oppressed, I flutter in bewilderment and fear.
Then crouch inert in darkness, grieving for the sun,
the radiance of open skies, inviting me
to be myself and fly.

    I cannot move. I feel
as if a mighty weight, annihilation's tool,
is crushing me, expelling life.

Here is no time. I die, but yet remain aware
I do not die. I live bereft of life.

Then, instant as your hand swept down,
it lifts and disappears.

Ah, Light! It cascades merrily
to fill the death-cell space with joy.
It warms my sun-starved, frozen form.

You cry, exulting, to me, "The time has come to fly,
you tiny aspect of my endless love!"
In one grand gesture then, you toss me upward
so I find my wings and what you made me for.
Intoxicated by such vastnesses of height and space
I dart and swoop
in ecstasies of flight.

The Voice

I was led down the path I had not chosen—
or, rather, I was drawn hypnotically.
One voice authoritatively announced,
"This is the way. Why do you linger? Move!"
Another seductively beguiled, "Don't listen."
It was the first I heeded. It gave me confidence.

Puzzling me, the signpost read, "Nothing and nowhere."
But the voice, now speaking in a foreign language,
urged me on. I recognized the intonation
though the words made nonsense. Then I asked myself,
"Who dares the wilderness alone, without a guide?"
And answered, "She who, hearing this discarnate voice, obeys."

The journey took me decades of hard labor.
"Here be wild beestes" some old signs read.
Encountered in ravines, these snarling creatures sprang
to savage me, or growled and backed away
because they heard the voice cry, "Go!"
At other times they crouched to lick my feet and hands.

Some terrors of the way were sensed, not seen.
Atavistic panic seized me in the dark.
I quaked and sweated, froze and churned; the shadows
sparkled with malignant eyes, hooked claws and teeth
that gleamed—a nameless, faceless Thing. I flinched—
then heard the steely voice, "I order you—go back to hell!"

I got so I could not believe this path—
obliterated as it often was by stones,

or halted like a crazy snake beside a precipice—
would ever lead me anywhere, and yet
I could not stop my legs' hypnotic motion
or my ears' compulsive listening for the voice.

And then one stygian night of deep, undreaming sleep
I heard it speak to me at last. Caress
of summer breeze was not more gentle. It said,
"Wake up, beloved. The long journey's over.
Open your bruised eyes, and gaze your fill of me."
I woke. I looked. I wept and laughed. I kissed my voice's mouth.

Connubial Blend

The cool, floating slabs of light calm
in the level sea
answer the evening sky.

"Are You there?"

"…Yes, I am here…"

"I move in undulations like soft, regular beats
of muffled drums reminding you how
my liquid nature, my mirror aptitude
reciprocates your every need, assuring you
of marital complicity to make two into one,
an interfusion of opposing elements—
air and water, light and all obscurities,
your unfortunate shortsightedness and my eternal wisdom,
your lackluster loving and my passionate embraces—
all in praxis to fulfil our marriage vows…

                              and then…

the being still together—
repose of mirrors
silence of drums
tranquillity of waters
do-nothing peace
connubial blend."

After Consecration

Easing myself into the peace
I slip over the brink of sleep,
into your arms. I lie there
my head against your breast
one hand at your heart's steady beat
the other crooked behind me
and all is quietude and still repose.
Your arms enfold me. They make a rampart
holding all my fears at bay.

Your breathing is the universe
you recreate each second through your love.
You are that mighty Word resounding
to make creation dance and sing in procreation.

Wedded for the first time in my life,
blessed, consecrated, vowed and ringed,
I now belong with you, love's circlet
mutual and pledged with sacramental grace.
Cherished and safe, cradled and defended
by the stronghold of your promise
I hold out in my trusting hand to you
all my love throughout eternity.

Lovers always say "for ever"—
and then betray each other.
But we have made our deathless troth
that enemies cannot destroy nor many waters quench
nor catastrophic earthquake turn to rubble.

Our "for ever" opens up eternity in us
where I lie cradled in your quiet arms
your steadfast heartbeat here beneath my hand
so that I believe, and trust, and render up my all
into your care whose dower is to me the universe.

Arrival and Indwelling

Through the aeons we have waited for each other—
"Before your mother's womb I knew you."

I believe you did—but I did not come to know you
until much later—and then gradually,
by means of stepping stones you yourself placed
here and there, each one a silent pledge
that neither quicksands, floods, earthquakes
or my own clumsy stumbling, would ever
dissociate my feet from your set plans for them.

I did get blisters though, and cuts both small and great—
a broken ankle once which you touched
with one fingertip for instant healing,
and then smiled in my eyes at my amazement.

Slowly, and at times in sudden gargantuan leaps
we ventured far into each other's inner fastnesses.

And I found out that at a certain stage
you never left me. You were there at home within me.
I was your dwelling place, and I became an adept
(through your personal help) at dwelling there
with you, contented, even blissful in that blessedness
you radiate to anyone and everyone who makes
the time and space to be with you, remaining so as to receive
whatever you may choose to send, and in whatever way.

Togetherness became so absolute it slipped one day
into that permanent marriage state that transformed me and all.
There was now no need for stepping stones. I had arrived.

Days of Grace

These translucent days slide in graced purpose
to their appointed end in future's crystal globe.

Whatever these days bring is blessed. And I, who do not know
how long my time here is to be
hold out receptive palms to rain or sun,
absorb through contemplative eyes
these oceanic vastnesses, these infinite skies
while on my brow is secretly impressed
the name I shall be called by
once these days are over.

When I watch pale primrose dawns ease up above the hill
all purity and calm, or the cloud pageant hues
shimmer in peacock and flamingo lakes of fire
and coruscating pools of silvery light
upon the sea's broad miles, I marvel.

Silence brims over, awe wells up,
hills crouch expectant, trees spread listening,
as invisible footsteps pass so close to me
my clay vibrates and trembles, and my palms
spread tight across my eyes
lest I be blinded by a glory
spilled out upon me now
before the hour appointed.

The blessing cup runs over
as far as the far rim of the turning world.

Betrothed Forever:
Risen With the Lord

Desert Call (Fall 1990)

The contemplative is not a special kind of person but everyone is—or ought to be—a special kind of contemplative. We must dispel our spooky notions of contemplation and realize that contemplation is for everyone: nurse, nun, monk, mother, or milkman.

The Holy Spirit is an expert explorer of the earthquake-prone ravines of our inner being. The process of deep spiritual cleansing she instigates and oversees far exceeds any psychological reorientation and integration induced through depth psychotherapy, though it bears resemblances to them and usually includes them to some degree as a by-product.

Whether experienced before or after death, this reassignment of things into right order involves a healing program for our spiritual ills that must be endured mostly in faith-filled passivity. There is little we can do except abandon ourselves and wait in what, if we persevere, will become heroic faith, hope, and love, while the Spirit secretly reorganizes our deepest selves and infuses those three special virtues into them. To stay open to this degree means, in Christocentric terms, accepting and living through, with and in him, the Lord's redemptive passion, crucifixion, death, and entombment. We have all been allotted a place in his life cycle, and if we merge perfectly with it, we fulfill his purposes for us.

If we remain faithful to the end, grace, having accomplished its purifying work, leads us out of spiritual entombment with Jesus into the love, joy, and fulfillment of his resurrection. We consented to stay with him to the end, and Scripture affirms that if we die with him we shall surely rise with him.

What does incorporation into the Lord's resurrection mean, and how does it affect us? Instead of generalizing, I shall in this article write in the first person, basing what I say on my own experience and its impact on me.

Emergence from entombment and identification with the crucified Lord happened for me on a precise date, my fiftieth birthday, which was twenty years ago. It initiated a startling switch from darkness into light, suffering into joy, deprivation into fulfillment, turmoil into peace, the sense of being abandoned and spurned by God into the awareness of entering the glorious liberty of his chosen children. Just as the crucifixion had happened in me with Jesus and for others, so did this resurrection and emergence from the tomb.

The stifling spiritual claustrophobia of the black cavern had changed within an hour to an unexpected, dramatically auspicious encounter with the dawn of a new life. It was a spiritual happening that was ineffable, yet poetic symbols of light, peace, beauty, and blessedness always come to me whenever I recall it.

It was as if I "saw" through Jesus' eyes creation's first pristine dawn when God said, "Let there be light!" and there was light. He had spoken the words once more for and in me, and now I was immersed in it—pellucid sky, silhouetted trees, a soft shining everywhere; quietness emphasized by the twitterings of waking birds; fresh, cool, pure air on my bruised face, bloodshot eyes, and aching brow; delicate, entrancing scents in my nostrils that had been filled with the stink of blood and death.

None of this was experienced through my senses. It was all interior, holy, spiritual—an ineffable mystery of grace. It was like waking up in heaven after a ghastly nightmare. Only analogies can convey some of its quality, and yet all these are inadequate. Being a writer, I attempt to make them.

I did not see the risen Lord in Gethsemane's garden with my bodily eyes or in my imagination. I did not "think it up." It was an interior happening directly impressed on my soul as a sacred, spiritual actuality—the risen Beloved's life-giving essence in terms of a new and eternal day—the everlasting life and Presence he had promised, encompassing and penetrating me in one rush of healing, invigorating grace. The certainty of being born again into a new dimension of being was overwhelming: "I have come that you might have life, and have it more abundantly."

What permanent effects has this gift of love—light and love— life from the risen Lord had on me and my life? One of the lasting ones has been a sense of glory—within myself and also permeating creation—eternal, not created glory. "The glory of the Lord fills the whole earth." I now know from personal experience that this is an actuality, the direct experience which increases awareness of the holiness of all God has made.

The book of Revelation tells us, "I saw there was no temple in the city, since the Lord God Almighty and the Lamb were themselves the temple" and we, too, are temples, of the Holy Spirit, "and the city did not need the sun or moon for light, since it was lit by the radiant glory of God and the Lamb was a lighted torch for it…. It will never be night again and [I shall] not need lamp-light or sunlight, because the Lord God is shining on [me]" (Rev. 21:22–23; 22:5).

The intense awareness of being inwardly bathed in the glory of the risen Lord lasted for some weeks, even months. After it faded, there remained, as it were, a holy afterglow like that in the western sky after sunset. During the following twenty years and until now the sense of being surrounded and permeated by this transfiguring light emanating from the risen Lord has remained with me almost constantly, usually muted, but occasionally vivid. I do not control it and can never either make it come or cause it to go. It is pure gift, as is the grace of Presence, of Trinitarian indwelling that infuses a sublimely gentle, indefinable peace. These remain permanently in my depths, whatever disturbances and trials occur in the upper levels of my mind and emotion.

This awareness of the glory of the risen Lord, his transfigured state and his inclusion of me in it, I understand to be one of the chief hallmarks of the born-into-new-life state of being. It confirms my faith that evil can never overcome or destroy what God has made and blessed, that Christ's redemptive work will never ultimately fail and that he calls me, all of us, to labor with him in it as our oblation of love and in gratitude for all he has done for us.

It assures me that God's love is warm, encompassing, reassuring, most beautiful, most holy, and that no hatred and malevolence can withstand it. Its incandescence will in the end blinds and annihilates all that oppose it, establishing the everlasting love-life of the risen Lord as the final and only reality.

The grace of personal, experiential certainty of the scriptural indwelling assures me in faith that even when I am physically alone (as I am for most of the time in my contemplative way of life), I am never alone.

For most of my life I had experienced myself as a piece of apparently lost luggage discovered at some foreign airport, owner unknown. Now Jesus had appeared to claim me, even openly demonstrating that his secret, baptismal sign of ownership had been indelibly printed on me long before, and no one could ever erase it. The conviction of having been at last finally claimed so that I now belonged in indissoluble union with someone who loved and wanted me, healed many ancient, suppurating emotional wounds, confirming my belief that grace can and does heal.

"I will betroth you to myself for ever, betroth you with integrity and justice, with tenderness and love" (Hos. 2:19).

Now God had ineradicably stamped my soul with his personal seal: "This is mine. No trespassing." I could joyously affirm with Paul, "I live—now not I, but Christ lives in me." Before my emergence from the tomb, I knew this in what might be called the negative, ego-elimination sense, as the suffering Christ including me in his passion that had as an integral part the desolating sense of being abandoned by God, even while bare faith unceasingly affirmed the opposite as the real truth. Though I experienced God as absent all those years, I never lost the conviction of the indwelling in me under the guise of the crucified Jesus living out his passion in me and my life. Because he was suffering in and with me, I was sustained, able to endure in his strength in the midst of my own weakness.

Now in the love-life of resurrection, the indwelling revealed itself as both different and similar. The Presence is now an entirely positive one, and though the risen Christ predominates; it is clearly Trinitarian as well, specifically with God as protective Abba and his Spirit as guide.

At this new level of being, the word "marriage" gains an infinitely richer significance because it is now a part of "eternal" life. In a sense it is according to the usual definition, an indissoluble union of "two in one flesh"—for I am definitely still in my fleshly body, and the Lord has made his home in me—though if a surgeon carved me up, he would not succeed in meeting Jesus.

He lives within me in a spiritual, immaterial way as surely as if he had made his home under my actual roof and ate with me at my actual dining table. He has remained with me not just as guest, but as permanent resident, lover, and spouse of my spirit (that deathless element within me) throughout the twenty years since that day when the stone was rolled away. And year after year he gains deeper possession of what is already his.

My awareness of Presence fluctuates. Mostly it is an arid, peaceful, almost humdrum certainty "in my bones," like the quiet acceptance and trust that permeates the relationship of an old, faithful, deeply bonded married couple. At rare times he graces me with a vivid, brief encounter—and eye to eye, face to face, as it were, but spiritual. There are never any "visions" as such. Mostly, he is "just there"—the rock bottom certainty and security of my life, the reason for all I do, am, love, and believe in—the purpose of every commitment.

The initial, dramatic liberation from all that had been oppressing and thwarting me (which I think of as the rolling away of the tomb's stone door) has evolved over the years into a continuous series of releases, small and large, as grace has prompted me to make further renunciations and ever deeper abandonments. These relinquishments are part of the permanent welding of my will to God's. This has occurred at ever-deepening levels, inducing "holy indifference," which means in itself more, not less, capacity for loving, because of less self-seeking. The only way I could have at any period dissolved this union would have been by the deliberate, death-dealing sin of repudiating him who has become my whole raison d'être. It is not, and has not been since my conversion, in my power to do this. I could and would never reject Jesus. He has all my love and life, my unconditional, permanent surrender to his ardent possession of me.

I am even more fundamentally certain he never can or will reject me. Possessed finally, I can no more make myself unpossessed than I can deny the fact that I exist. All I want now is to be used by him for as long as we are together on this earth and into eternity.

He came to lead me out of death into his own everlasting life. I long to be one of his instruments in his work of bringing the whole of humanity into the final consummation of the love-life of his resurrection in each one of us, his multitudinous beloveds. I want my daily existence to be nothing but him, living and acting, loving and giving, through me. The awareness of being his channel, his instrument, his other self, has at times been overwhelming during these last twenty years. It fills me with humility and awe, though he seldom shows me where or how, and in relation to whom, he has used and is using me. I am glad he "hides me in the shadow of his wings," for I do not want to fall into the trap of congratulating myself that I (the big Ego, the self-seeking, false me) am accomplishing anything for the kingdom by myself. Without Christ, I could and can do nothing, but with him, my will welded into his, anything is possible.

The results are his business. I plod on in blind faith and trust when I cannot understand what he is doing with my life, and through me to others who are part of it. At rare times he seems to take me with him on some errand of mercy, while bodily I remain right where I am, with a peculiar yet unshakable certainty that "virtue has gone out of me" but under his control and for his purposes, to someone else who, usually, I do not even know.

He is using me, this assures me, for one tiny part of his healing and redeeming of humanity—as long as I let him, as long as my will remains open to his unchecked invasion of me. And I "see" how he is also doing this with countless other people, some unaware of it, others aware to greater or lesser degrees—anyone and everyone who trustfully says yes to him.

Another grace of the love-life of his resurrection that he has given me is the direct experience of what it is like to drink his living waters constantly from the fountain of his love. The result is that now, in this state, I am never thirsty and desert-bound as for so many years I was, as I cried out from our cross, "I thirst!" He has taken away my sins, birthed me in his Spirit, given me eternal life and bread from heaven, buried me in his will (which is to do the will of his Father), poured out for me from his own heart the fountains of inner healing, given me his truth that has made me free, become my gate to go in and out of in certain safety, lifted me up from the earth with himself (first on a cross, then into his own ascension and resurrection glory—invisible yet there within my secret self), and given me his indestructible peace that the world can never provide. At the same time as he exalts and enriches me, he shows me constantly how empty, poor, and helpless I am, and this in itself is a very special, precious grace, for the poorer I am, the more richly he will endow me.

What can I give him in return? Only my whole heart, my will down to its unconscious depths, for him to use—the how, when, where, why, and to whom of it entirely at his disposal.

"Behold, I have come to do your will." This is the essence of being risen with the Lord—to be unreservedly at his disposal forever. And the motive? Nothing but love. Of him. Of every neighbor and each enemy. And to grow in that love each day by deeper abandonment to his own love pouring into the stretched-wide human heart.

"It is to the glory of my Father that you should bear much fruit, and then you will be my disciples.... Remain in my love.... You did not choose me. No—I chose you, and I commissioned you to go out and bear fruit, fruit that will last" (John 15).

All of us have been given him by the Father. His desire is to love each of us into the love-life of his resurrection, so that we can uninhibitedly do this work with him. Then he is glorified in us, and we in him.

Only in this way can the world be saved—using the word "saved" in every possible sense. It is imperative that each of us goes up to Jerusalem to be crucified and entombed with him, so that we will rise with him and be put to work to produce fruits for eternity. Only these can save our afflicted planet and all its peoples.

"As you sent me into the world, I have sent them into the world" (John 17:18). I would say one of the plainest hallmarks of being risen to the new life of glory is this humble conviction of being "sent" to "bear fruit"—the fruit that Jesus himself labored for and desires above all—the salvation of every human being who has ever lived or will live on this earth.

Puny and powerless though I know I am, I also know the force of a nuclear explosion is stored in a spiritual way in the Lord living in me. The more I remain receptive to his usage, the more docile to his demands, the more tuned in through prayer and love to his Spirit, the more disinterested in my motives—the more freely and far-reachingly he can use me. My certainty of this is so deep that it is now for me part of "common sense"—that innate understanding of "how life really is" that stops us from doing silly things while it prompts us to act in more appropriate ways.

The Spirit's wisdom about the divine Life of the world—Jesus here and now, in dynamic operation, in control, behind (and also through) all the absurdities and calamities while also ready to activate me and all others who wish to be used by him for his own redeeming purposes—is what the risen Lord in me affirms as truth. I do not have to understand. All I need to do is keep myself unreservedly at his disposal. Then—sleeping or waking, writing or weeding the garden, talking or listening, comforting or cajoling, praying or observing, ill or well, alone in my poustinia or participating in family activities—he is living in and through me and so using me for others.

This is what the love-life of his resurrection is given for—to be the yeast in the dough, the salt in the stew. It is the life that is the light of the world, the light shining in the dark and never being overpowered by it. He has lit us as his lamps and placed us on the lampstand of his loving will. Now he directs our mutual light wherever he wants it to shine, and though we may never see the one it illuminates and that person never knows of our existence, it does not concern us.

To be used by the risen Lord in his resurrection work of love and healing is all that matters. This is his great grace to those he leads by the hand out of entombment into his own risen love-life and everlasting glory.

Grace Given

You drench me in your blessedness—
pressed down, compacted, flowing over,
till here I am, a child caught in a storm of love,
saturated with these discarnate ecstasies.

Your ways are masterful. Your generosity,
now captive in my starveling heart, loads me
with luxurious garments, crown and jewels—
treasures gained by you in times long past,
and yet enduring into our eternal now.

You are willing captive to my abject,
but trustingly prosaic, homeliness.

Where do we go from here?
Into some fastness of delight and fortitude,
a refuge for those wanderers, besotted by your love?

I cannot conceive (nor do I try)
what you have in store for me, but rest
in faith's patient hope, and love's fierce faith.

It is you who taught me how to love—
assiduous, recklessly adventurous
and all the while imprisoned deep
within your mighty stronghold of a heart.

The Wings of God

The wings that stretched the heavens like clouds
I climbed upon. And long
and ardently they bore me in their easeful flight.
They were strong.
Fireless they were—I was a puny burden,
no more than dust.
The long, smooth surge I rested on became
my final trust.

The heavens' span and all the wide, thronged space
of universes
is to these wings
an habitable room, a stretching place for leisurely tours
and comfortable journeyings.
What, now that I have cast myself upon their strength,
have I to fear?
And yet my heart is humbled into awe
to be so near.

Prayer Time

The traffic goes on and on.
Talk about rush hour!

    Lord,
I don't want it to be this way,
I long for stillness for both of us,
for us to meet and embrace in a holy emptiness
filled with your Spirit. I don't want
these endless, trivial interruptions,
these mundane comments, this sheer nonsense—
like confetti thrown all over us
as we walk away from the consecration
of our nuptials, into the world and our work there.

You are very patient. You take no notice
of my repetitive slogans. My captive mind
that reiterates so boringly these matters of no moment
and dallies down side roads
looking at silly signposts and place names,
seeming to disregard you.

    I say "seeming"
for all the time I am so deeply and intricately
intertwined with you, so absolutely yours,
(as you are mine) that there's no separation now
for all eternity.

Amen, and Alleluia.

Christ, the Vocation

Cross and Crown (December 1970)

For the last fifteen years or so, I have been in a situation that the phrase "neither fish nor fowl" describes nicely. I should like to elaborate on it in a personal way, because I fancy that in this age of change, bewilderment, confusion, and contradiction, my situation and what I have made of it may be relevant, with some changes of labels, to others who may have the nagging sense that they "don't belong anywhere."

Not so long ago I announced exasperatedly to a priest, "I'm neither wife, virgin, nor widow. The only thing that can be said for certain about me is that I'm a mother!" He exasperated me further by laughing and telling me this was a grace.

Why did I say this?

Well, I am fifty and the facts are these: (1) a civil marriage long ago, that I had no intention of being permanent, for I then believed in "trial marriages"; and (2) the bearing of three children that undeniably made me a mother.

Conversion to Christianity, and then to Catholicism in my mid-thirties, brought the realization of what true marriage meant. I made a sincere effort to rescue our marriage, but my husband, moved by some irrational, fierce compulsion beyond his control, declared that Catholicism made me completely and finally repulsive to him.

When all attempts at reconciliation failed and I actually entered the Church, the end of our marriage followed.

There ensued painful, harassed years of intolerable stress and strain. I had to return to the profession I had been trained for, teaching, and work to keep the home going and see my children educated. There was the hideous loneliness, condensed in the fashionable phrase, "single parent," the cross branded deep and ineradicably, the sense of belonging nowhere and with no one. This was eased by the affirmation of ever-deepening and ever-tried faith that I did belong in Christ's Church and with him. He was my Beloved, my Lord, the whole reason for my existence. As I struggled to find a true vocation in something, interior or exterior, this belonging-to-Christ remained the one stable factor.

Was my vocation to be a mother? How could it be when circumstances forced me to work full time, and a separation agreement and an embittered father ensured that my children could never follow me into the Church. Love them and labor for them as I might, there was a deep cleavage in fundamental understanding and fusion that affection just could not bridge.

To help the mentally and emotionally afflicted? For many years in my earlier life I had studied and labored to prepare myself for work as a lay psychotherapist. My intense compassion for and understanding of the interior sufferings of human beings, and the fact that many people affirmed the reality of my help, made me certain I had a vocation to serve and heal in this field. However, the collapse of my personal life through the events of my conversion eliminated a budding career. Whatever tentative efforts I made after entering the Church to renew it met with familiar failure.

To be a teacher then? Certainly I reveled in the work and the classroom relationships, but just as certainly it drained me into idiotic exhaustion. There was little chance of making it a "career," or even a serious job, for my health refused to stand up to it and periodic rests were essential.

A kind of perennial student? In times between teaching I completed an Arts degree with such high marks that first class honors seemed sure to follow. But no—God's recipe was not to be diluted. Circumstances conspired to leave me with only upper second class honors. Thus a lecturing position, or a scholarship to do higher research, was rendered impossible. Vocation in the academic world, then, much as I thrived on and loved the exhilarating exercise of my mind, was not to be mine.

Writing—my lifelong love? Were I to count the hours of dedicated, passionate work spent on my writing ever since I was little more than a child, and then balance it against financial rewards and literary recognition, the results would be profoundly depressing. Just as well that I write primarily for the sheer, creative joy of it. Nevertheless, publication is sought, because one writes to communicate. Yet, though I have had some hundreds of pieces of various kinds published in different countries and since becoming a Catholic—two books (which have both been market failures)—I have found it quite impossible to earn my living at writing, no matter how hard I work. As I was forced by my nonvocation of being neither wife, virgin, nor widow to earn my living, writing seemed out as a vocation, in the sense of a full-time occupation.

The religious life? Surely that was the obvious solution for one crazy enough to become a Catholic in the face of such opposition and in the midst of such retaliations. Surely that was the sensible thing for one whose whole life month by month, year by year, came more and more under the dominion of Christ through conviction, dedication, and grace. Ah, but what about the mother? She has children to bring up, and now that at last they are launched, she is fifty, and her health would never stand up to the regimen. So vocation to the religious life is out too.

What is left?

Nothing much really. It is true that every attempt I have made (and there are numbers of minor ones not listed here) to discover

God's will in some kind of clearly defined vocation through which I could give my life to him and serve others for his sake has been thwarted.* Failure has been the most consistent brand on my life. Thus, it has always amused me when people go on about my "achievements."

True achievement is knowing you are doing what God wants you to do, and doing it in utter dedication and love for his sake. In short, achievement lies in a discovered and fulfilled vocation.

A Happy Discovery

All through the years, one of my deepest and most constant griefs was the sense of not having this vocation. But now the grief has been assuaged. Replacing it is a quietly radiant happiness, a calm certainty of having at last found my niche.

How has this come about?

There is one word that covers it all: "Christ," and yet elaboration is necessary to show how and why.

My conversion was certainly what the devotional books call "a love affair with Jesus." Only those who have really gone through this experience can know that there is a sense in which the phrase has not the least sentimentality about it, but is, instead, the most exact way to describe an indescribable process of absolute change.

It was the summons of the personal Christ, personally known and personally loved that led me into his Church. He said to me, a person, by name Barbara, as he said to Philip, Peter, James, John, and the rest, "Come, follow me." And just as they responded without the least hesitation because their hearts knew he was the Lord, so did I. It was impossible to do anything else. His influence is hypnotic, when you meet him person-to-person. "Deep calls unto deep," and the spontaneous reply is, "Yes, Lord. I'm coming. Right now."

That simply is the way it affected me.

Key Doctrines

Since my life was clearly Christ-branded before I even knew Catholicism, it is understandable that the two doctrines of the Church that drew me most persistently were those of the real presence and the mystical body. God sealed my intellectual knowledge of these with certain graces of faith and love so that they began, and have continued, to shape my whole life. Initial insights and graces were followed by progressively deepening ones over the years, until the whole universe is, for me, clearly the expression of Christ, the Word uttered by God, the channel through whom all things were made and in whom they find their essential being.

"Christ is!" seems to me the liturgical chant of creation, and the Mass and the Eucharist fasten this eternal, infinite paean into time and place.

✳ I knew when I was received into the Church that I was received into Christ and that Christ was received into me through the sacraments, and especially the Eucharist. So intense was this realization that it dictated my life as a Catholic from the beginning. The one thing I knew for sure that God wanted of me became impressed on me like a seal at my very first Mass and Communion. He wanted me, every day, to be a stand-in, a proxy, for all those who could not, or would not, unite themselves to Christ in his act of immolation, worship, love, and reconciliation made continually through his priests at the altar.

✳ The Mass was the lifeline of the world. To identify myself with Christ in it for the sake of the world was the most powerful means at my disposal for helping others. Christ wanted to extend himself throughout the world by means of Christians, and the more fully he was present in me, the more completely he would be able to use me. Therefore, I must be fed with "the living bread" that I might become his perfect instrument.

✳ This summons to daily Mass and Communion, in clear knowledge that it was not just for my good but for that of all humanity, was the basis of what I now, at last, recognize and embrace as my vocation. It was, from the beginning, apostolic.

Suffering Love

In my early years in the Church, grace prompted me to seal my pact, my gift of my whole self to Christ for his work in the world, by certain vows and pledges, personal and peculiar to me and my way of life. These intimately concerned what I call "suffering-love." They arose from my experiential realization that it was through his passion and death that Christ redeemed the world. All my suffering (and the load of it, through interior and exterior circumstances, was so crushing that day by day, hour by hour, I knew I survived only by means of the graces I received through my daily Mass and Communion) was meaningful as part of his redemptive act.

The suffering of Christ-in-me was his loving of the world through me. There was no better nor more creative way in which I could reach out to and help the world than by this suffering love in union with him. The deeper my realization of this truth became, the more suffering seemed to come to me, and with it a more intense experience of union with Christ.

At the same time, I was involved directly with people, mainly through the classroom, but also in other ways more commonly regarded as "apostolic activities." I certainly wanted with my whole heart to be used by God and yet, as I have already demonstrated, every time I said to myself, "Ah, this is it!" and threw myself into it, the result was rejection or defeat or a conspiracy of circumstances that made it impossible to continue.

In the middle of all this came Vatican II, with its inspiring reorientation toward the contemporary world. Its stress on the role of the laity as renewers of the temporal order, those with a vocation to make Christ present wherever their work and life took them in modern society, seemed to give official blessing to those interior trends already present in me. For the first time, after pondering over the conciliar decrees on the Church, on the Church in the modern world, and on the laity, I realized that lay life could really be a vocation, a calling, in the true sense of the word. The documents' stress on the laity's role of "consecrating the world itself to God" by "engaging in temporal affairs and by ordering them according to the plan of God" (*Dogmatic Constitution on the Church*, n. 31) made sense to me. It also removed the idea that lay life was only second best to religious life.

✳ I had all along been conscious that Christ wanted to make of me a ciborium, a monstrance, a chalice, a pyx, in which he could be borne to people; now the Church was defining and elaborating on this role. There was no need to wear a habit or enter the enclosure to carry it out. It was an essential part of ordinary daily living right in the world. After Vatican II, I dedicated myself to my professional work and told God I was willing to renounce solitude and silence for the rest of my life in order to take my part in "consecrating the world itself," in truly embracing my vocation as a lay person and a teacher.

The only result was a continuation of the familiar seesaw pattern. Then, some months ago, this culminated in a physical collapse through overwork and overstrain plus the accumulation of the years of suffering. It became quite plain the work was beyond me, and that therefore it could not be God's will for me. From now on my "work in the world" would be desultory and part-time and only when financial straits compelled it. The life of solitude and silence that I had always longed for had at last become a necessity for reasons of health. God had made his point—but among all the contradictions, it was some time before I clearly understood what that point was.

I think that often we are prompted by grace to do and say things whose full significance we do not discover for years afterward. The final discovery reveals the pattern made by divine Providence. I begin now to see such a pattern.

"Doing" Issues From "Being"

All my life I had been aware that the sources of our actions are deep within ourselves: "doing" issues from "being." As a Catholic, I knew from the first that the interior life was all-important, and this made me certain that I could not spread love or do good in the world except through the power of Christ present in me. I must be a vessel pouring him out. I had to "be" before I could "do" in helping to establish the kingdom of heaven on earth.

However, in spite of this, and also because of the emphasis in our Western philosophy and way of life on "doing," I kept on trying to find a vocation in something that would show obvious and measurable results in terms of human achievement. My lack of success resulted in certain important inner developments that greatly aided me in the final discovery of my true vocation.

✶ My inability to fit in anywhere led to an increasing awareness of being, as St. Paul says, "a tent dweller." It deepened my faith and hope that my home was not here, but in heaven. It prevented me from attaching myself to human organizations, pursuits and works (however good and worthy) for their own sakes.

✶ Being forced to keep on the move, as it were, I had to abandon all but the essentials, to travel light, to remember the basic truths of Christian living and not get involved in secondary issues. More and more, success, position, money, recognition, importance, praise, possessions, and labels meant less and less to me. God's action producing the series of failures in my life lessened my self-importance and forced me to cultivate detachment and ironic insight into the hollowness of nearly all that is regarded as worth striving for and clinging to once attained.

The contradictions thrown up in my path left me no option but to rely in blind faith on divine Providence, to affirm that every disaster would bring eventual good for me and others. The darkness that he cast upon my soul and my life was intensified by the inability to find help in any human agent, and this in itself was a grace.

The pattern of sense began to emerge from the nonsense when I saw, about eighteen months ago now, how those early offerings and vows I had made under the promptings of grace had really been the cause of all that had happened to me since. They were the key to meaning. In and by them I had sought to open the way more completely for Christ to take possession of me that he might live in me for the sake of the world. All that God had let happen to me had really been his answer to my prayer of longing for Christ expressed in those pledges.

I began to see how everything fitted together. Vatican II gave a specific vocation to the lay person. It made me happy to be Christ in the world, but God meant the emphasis for me personally to be far more on the "be" than on the "world." This was fully in keeping with what my deepest spiritual intuitions and inclinations had been all along.

It was not something odd and extraordinary that he asked of me; on the contrary, it was the true, basic vocation for every Christian, lay or religious, married or single, young or old. This basic vocation for all of us is to extend the Incarnation, to be a witness for Christ right where we are.

✴ When St. Thérèse discovered her vocation, "I will be love in the heart of the Church," she saw it as being inclusive of all others. In some such way I saw the vocation that God had given me of "being Christ in the world" as somehow embracing all others.

He was not calling me to strive against social injustices, nurse the sick, keep the economy going, enter politics, or do any other of the innumerable tasks and works humans as social beings have to perform. He was calling me fundamentally to be a witness to Christ by being the suffering-loving-praying Christ, hidden and alone, like a secret powerhouse concealed in some cleft in the mountains, yet still part of human society.

✴ The sense of rightness and release at this discovery of vocation was tremendous. For the first time in my life I felt I was truly and completely my individual self; my identity was discovered.

Channel of Christ's Grace

"Therefore, the apostolate of the Church and of all its members is principally directed toward witnessing Christ to the world by word and action, and by serving as a channel of his grace" (*Decree on the Apostolate of the Laity*, n. 6).

"Channel of his grace" is my key phrase. I am not called "to immerse myself directly and decisively in the secular order" (Ibid., n. 7).

I tried that, but God put an end to it. I am called to witness to the spiritual reality that must be behind and permeating all such immersions. I am called to a direct involvement with Christ as a living sign that only from such involvement can the right, God-directed kind of involvement with society develop.

My primary apostolate and true vocation is to "be." Every Christian has to be Christ where Christ wishes to be in him. This apostolate is independent of outward circumstances and additional vocations of work or service imposed upon it. The vocation to be Christ, the "channel of his grace," precedes and supersedes all other vocations, making them always secondary.

Perhaps a clearer realization of this basic truth that I am called upon to witness to in a concentrated fashion as my personal vocation will help those troubled by restlessness, doubt, and change.

I hope my story will bring peace and meaning to some who feel that the familiar handholds have been snatched away and that they are left spinning above an abyss of unmeaning. In the heart of all change abides the eternally changeless, Christ himself, Master and Lord. He calls each one of us to be an extension of his incarnation, to be personally involved with him, to be his good and his love in the world. This is the common vocation for all Christians, uniting us in one loving, eternally relevant purpose.

The Source

I have a shrine within me.
Tapers burn there day and night
flowers gather round the candles—
colors and living flames
mingle in extravagance of bloom,
celebrating love and chastity.

I meet you here in stillness.
my head against your tranquil heart
bends in homage, rests in peace;
my own heart dares to merge
with that unquenchable furnace from which
we both derive our reckless gift of self.

This is the living flame of love,
this is the source of primal energy,
of every urge to impetuous offering
of myself. Here, with bowed head
and face against your breast
I drink the strength I need, and give my all.

Tuning In

The resounding silence of your presence
encloses and permeates me. A symphony
of murmurs that mean everything and nothing,
what preceded music in primitive harmonies.
I tune in—as best I can. Listening intently
I begin to hear your messages that, coded, mean so much.

The narrow aperture I have for getting in and out
enlarges of its own accord, its receptivity increases,
transmitting into me truths I once half comprehended
and now transpose and understand as if spoken
in my mother tongue and transcribed by a master of the task.

The Beggar's Song

Whatever the weather, I'll sing Amen—
a statement pithy and to the point.
The sound of it appeals to me
in my attenuated circumstances.

When the wind's wintry whistle penetrates
my tattered garments that once
were velvet, adorned with intricate embroidery
gold thread, pouches and pockets, all
in the latest fashion, and costing most
of what I earned—when that wind now
accurately locates each thin, worn place,
each rent and hole, each buttonless gap
and infiltrates them all with icy torrents of air—
then I gambol on the frosty grass, capering
to keep myself alive, though I do admit it is
also to indicate to all that I am frolicking.
Amen to this also—the latest
of your gifts of love and grace.

Now I have no home except in you.
I wander country roads, sleep rough,
beg my food, drink when it rains, thirst
in the heat. I see dawn, sunrise, noon, sunset,
and thus I learn how blind I was before
when I had walls about me and a roof
sturdy to shut out stars and full moon's glare,
all conversations with all luminaries
banished finally in favor of unstructured space.

And so I sing Amen and laugh aloud
rejoicing in my penury. People judge me
mad but harmless.
        Perhaps I am, and so
I sing amen to that as well.

The Poustinia Way

New Zealandia (date unknown)

It was Harry who gave me a copy of Catherine de Hueck Doherty's *Poustinia*. What this Russian woman described provided both enrichment and verification of the lifelong urge deep within me compelling me to seek solitude, silence, and God's presence wherever I was living or working.

She writes: "In the Western sense of the word 'poustinia,' it would mean a place to which a hermit goes and, hence, it could be called a hermitage."

> The word to the Russian means much more than a geographical place that people wish to enter, to find the God who dwells within them. It also means truly isolated, lonely places to which specially called people would go as hermits, and would seek God in solitude, silence, and prayer for the rest of their live…. It was considered a definite vocation, a call from God to go into the "desert" to pray to God for one's sins and the sins of the world. Also, to thank him for the joys and the gladness and all his gifts. (Doherty, *Poustinia*, 30–31)

In my fifties, about the time I read the book, I was put on a medical benefit that led to my automatically receiving the Age Benefit a couple of years early. At last I had a meager but certain income and no longer needed to stay near schools where I could obtain spasmodic work and pay as a substitute teacher.

I could do what my heart constantly longed for—leave the city and head for the wilds.

For months I prayed and searched diligently for a place within my limited means and isolated enough to be a genuine poustinia. I had no success and, discouraged, almost decided this could not be, after all, a genuine call from God. He was just playing with me to test my abandonment. Then February came, and I planned a camping break at Piha after the holiday crowds were gone. Before I went, I searched, as usual, in the "Properties for Sale" column in the *Herald*, just in case—and there was a cottage listed at Piha and priced within my means.

I rang the owner, found it was unoccupied, was told its location and where to find the key, and set off, trying to control the unruly hope surging up in me.

What I found was the plain answer to my longings and my prayers.

High on a hill above the road, isolated, with huge macrocapas about it, framing a magnificent ocean, coastal, farmland and Waitakere Range views, was this unassuming little fibrolite cottage with its ample, timbered front deck facing due north and the beach far below. Tiny, but unexpectedly tasteful and sensibly planned inside, with natural timber walls and built-in kauri table and servery, plus superb views out every window, it was just about everything I had longed for and almost given up hope of finding.

Moreover, as the owner had been trying to sell it for a year or two and was eager to get rid of it, he was willing to drop his price so that I still had enough capital left to have a large studio with bedroom and a small back porch built on. When

I moved in, I asked God to let me live there till I died. Later, a brain tumor prevented this prayer from being answered, but, before I had to leave, I had six blissful years of hermit life that were sheer "uninterrupted blessedness." This phrase that came to me then perfectly summarizes the grace peculiar to a poustinia vocation fulfilled. From my eyrie I looked out daily upon such panoramic vistas reflecting the glory, grandeur, and beauty of God's creation that they seemed the source of a constant alleluia chant. This was expressed also through nature's sounds in the macrocapas, bird calls, lowing cattle from the farm down the road, possums chittering in the night, owls' eerie hooting, far whispers from the surf below, rain on my roof, and the uproar of winter gales and storms.

All these blessed my ears as the visual beauty blessed my eyes. It was as if, constantly held out to me, Jesus' hands were overflowing with gifts most likely to delight me.

I was never lonely in my aloneness with God in my poustinia. Day and night were permeated with a ceaseless, usually silent prayer of worship, peace, gratitude, and fulfillment. It was automatically offered up with and to Jesus for our wounded and reeling world and all the suffering human beings on it—those he longs to permeate with his saving love, only too often it is resisted and scorned. I explored the bush tracks with my dog, walked or drove down the steep, winding road to the beach to swim or walk its long, empty stretch the whole length, the wind in my hair, my dog chasing seagulls, their cries and the crash of the surf in my ears, a paean of praise in my heart.

When the holiday crowds came, I stayed way above them all in my eyrie, and solitude and silence preserved.

My days were full of creativity that was also prayer. I wrote, studied, painted, took up weaving and patchwork, sewed. Outside I labored to grow a garden on the rough, clay slopes and leveled patches. I planted flowers and vegetables, dug with shovel, fork, and grubber for the gorse and bracken. I felt well and strong, sweated, heaved, and thoroughly enjoyed myself. My vegetables tasted all the better for the effort that had gone into producing them. And my flowers were special prayers of love and gratitude.

Those years alone with God on top of a remote hill surrounded by scrub, second-growth native shrubs and trees, macrocapas and incredible views, have left embedded in my memory and heart a shrine of holiness steeped in the presence of the Creator whose gift of love and blessing they were to me in return for the gift of my heart to him to use as he pleased.

It was always clear in my mind that the poustinia way and vocation of Spirit-permeated solitude and silence was to make its practitioner a channel through which healing and blessing sent by God could flow invisibly to others. One became an anonymous transmitter, a tool for Christ to use how and for whom he chose in his redemptive work for humanity.

The power of prayer is immeasurable, and those called to the poustinia way have this hidden-away-with-Christ-in-God vocation. They are called to live in a state of constant prayer of the heart for anyone and everyone, usually unaware of who it is God is using them for, but believing in faith that they are being used.

✶ It broke my heart when the secret enemy in my brain and its physical effects in my body made it impossible for me to live any longer so alone and so far away from any help—but I have kept my poustinia vocation inviolate in my heart ever since. Though my present hermitage is not situated in such remote seclusion, it has been carefully chosen so solitude and silence and awareness of God's presence can be preserved.

✷ After all, the true poustinia is always within, where our union with God is alive and active. The hidden solitude and silence of a will and heart given unreservedly to him denote the indestructible, invisible poustinia of the heart not made with hands. Without this no material poustinia can be a genuine one. The inner one can exist whether we live in a hospital bed in a busy ward; in a flat in a crowded high-rise building above a busy city street; in a home brimming with the intermingling family relationships of husband, wife, and a clutch of children; or alone in an isolated cottage above the ocean high on a Piha hill.

The 1983 Canon Law provision for lay hermits, section 603, states:

> Besides institutes of consecrated life, the Church recognizes the life of hermits or anchorites, in which Christ's faithful withdraw further from the world and devote their lives to the praise of God and the salvation of the world in the silence of solitude and through constant prayer and penance.
>
> Hermits are recognized by law as dedicated to God in consecrated life if, in the hands of the diocesan Bishop, they publicly profess, by a vow or some other sacred bond, the three evangelical counsels, and then lead their particular form of life under the guidance of the diocesan bishop.

When I read this canon I knew it was for me and this had been, and was to be, and is, my vocation till I die, no matter where circumstances force me to live.

Eve Redeemed

Eve
these days you are so tranquil.
I see you sitting there before your cave
for hours, looking out to sea
to where the two horizons merge
—sky and ocean—and infinity begins.

Eve
sometimes I wonder if you're ill
but then I sense the peace that emanates
from your still form. I meet your eyes
and in them find such depths of quietude
I marvel, remembering certain tumults of the past.

Eve
when was it that the miracle occurred?
That day I told you to put on
your girdle of dried grasses,
to make some order in your matted hair
and come with me to meet the Three?

Eve
you were so docile as you sat just where
I told you to, at Jesus' feet. His hand
was on your wayward head, he smiled—
and I saw tears well up and fill your wary eyes
that met and lost themselves in His.

Eve
that day was when you changed—
my sister and my other self, so often in the past
my tribulation and embarrassment, now
all made new, your eyes upon infinity
your wayward heart throbbing the one word, Love.

Alone With The Alone

I am a quiet person. Sometimes you may hear music
of a special kind, or my dog barking
at a suspected intruder (who seldom materializes)
but little else.

Here on my hill, near the top,
sundry noises ascend from the flat—
its conglomeration of dwellings, its roads,
its sounds of busy building of new houses
and of children playing, shouting, laughing.
But here—only the myriad birds in springtime ecstasy
singing from the totaras, calling in celebration of life.
And the silence of God's Presence, his approaches
without fanfare, but steeped in actuality,
and with a quiet (and inevitable) strength of purpose,
until arrival is consummated in that unique blending.

I live alone with the Alone (my dog and cat
do not intrude!). And I am glad
the radio is silent except for brief news bulletins
and there is no television—(I gave it away)—
and the world goes on its chaotic lurching about
oblivious of me and my unobtrusive ways.

I rejoice in solitude and silence and regard
the far-off hills, the verdant pastures, trees and hedges
with appreciative eyes that linger on the contours
God molded in a past long gone, yet present,
in this everlasting now of peace and beauty's gifts.

Living in the Darkness

Entombment and Resurrection

Cross and Crown (March 1964)

"For in this sepulchre of dark death it must needs abide until the spiritual resurrection which it hopes for" (*Dark Night* 2:2).

The mysteries of our Lord's life are continually being reenacted through the liturgy of his Church and also in the interior lives of individual Catholics. This could scarcely be otherwise, considering the extension of the mystical body through time. Christ lives on in us and—during, before, and after our lives—in his Church, not as an inanimate statue, but as a palpable being, incarnated over and over in human beings.

It follows that what our Lord was and is, we are—to the extent that we fulfill his destiny for us by entering into union with him. "It is now no longer I who live, but Christ lives in me" (Gal. 2:20). No one can tell to what extent Christ lives in him, but the yearning to be fully possessed must be the energizing force in Christian day-to-day existence.

Because Christ is infinite and eternal, his manhood and his Godhead and all the mysteries of his life are always present in him outside the restrictions of time. But we, as mortal beings, are confined in this life in linear time, and consequently our participation in his mysteries is not a simultaneous whole, but a fragmentary progression. Yet at the same time there can be a curious telescoping, so that even as we wait for the Advent mystery to take place in our own souls ("Come and bring forth from the dungeon the prisoner sitting in darkness and the shadow of death"), we know that it has already taken place, for by baptism we were brought out of the darkness and illuminated with the light that is everlasting. This waiting-to-be and this having-already-become are mysteriously intertwined throughout the spiritual life, so that often it is quite impossible to say that one state exists or one thing is happening to the exclusion of the other. And when one pauses to think, this is just what might be expected, for by baptism we are incorporated into the whole Christ—Christ in all his mysteries enacted on this earth; Christ in glory now that he is risen; and Christ who already was the Word at the beginning of time, and without whom was made nothing that has been made. The life that is in us is especially the life of the risen Christ—Christ in glory, Christ triumphant, Christ the beginning and the end, Christ the temple of heaven. "I saw no temple therein. For the Lord God almighty and the Lamb are the temple thereof. And the city has no need of the sun or moon to shine upon it. For the glory of God lights it up, and the Lamb is the lamp thereof" (Rev. 21:22–23).

Consequently, the life of Christ in a soul in the state of grace is a life of glory, no matter what that soul's subjective experiencing of its state may be. It was her deep insight into this mystery that gave Blessed Elizabeth of the Trinity her spiritual raison d'être and was the source of her beautiful teaching:

> "The heavens declare the glory of God." The glory of God: that is what the heavens proclaim, and as my soul is a heaven where I dwell while awaiting the heavenly Jerusalem, this heaven too must proclaim the glory of the Eternal, *nothing* but the glory of the Eternal. In the heaven of our soul, let us be praises of glory of the Blessed Trinity, and praises of love of our Immaculate Mother. One day the veil will drop, we shall be led into the eternal courts; and then we shall sing in the bosom of infinite love. God will give us the

new name promised to those who win victory. What
will it be? Laudem Gloriae. (Philipon, *Spiritual Writings*, 163, 153)

Price of Sharing Christ's Risen Life

Although this heavenly glory is present in every soul that is in
a state of grace, it cannot be fully entered into or claimed except
by conscious and willing participation in all the mysteries of
Christ's life.

"The Spirit himself gives testimony to our spirit that we are
the children of God. But if we are children, we are heirs also:
heirs indeed of God and joint heirs with Christ, provided, however, we suffer with him that we may also be glorified with him"
(Rom. 8:16–17).

Just as the oak tree is incipient in the acorn, so the glorious life
of the risen Christ is incipient in the soul of the baptized Christian,
but to come to its full stature it must be cultivated deliberately and
consistently through the practice of virtue and sacramental graces.
This is glibly said, but it can be achieved only through bitter pain.
The higher the state of glory to be attained, the fiercer will be the
battle and the anguish. In his wonderful passage on the interior life
of the victorious Christian, St. Paul says, "We know that all creation groans and travails in pain until now. And not only it but we
ourselves also who have the first-fruits of the Spirit—we ourselves
groan within ourselves, waiting for the adoption as children, the
redemption of our body" (Rom. 8:22–23).

The slavery from which we are redeemed is our immersion in
time, our bondage of concupiscence, our wound of original sin, our
vulnerability to the devil. Our spirits, confined in our traitorous
bodies with all their clamorous needs and their seductive urges,
cannot rest for an instant. Our whole life long, we are in either a
state of siege or a battle to the death. No wonder we "groan within

ourselves" as we try to lift ourselves up to that heaven that seems
so unattainable but so desirable.

And yet it is already within us! "The kingdom of God is within
you" (Luke 17:21). St. Paul comforts us:

> Now [that is, throughout all this wearisome struggle
> and waiting, this paradoxical having and not having]
> we know that for those who love God all things work
> together unto good, for those who, according to his
> purpose, are saints through his call. For those whom he
> has foreknown he has also predestined to become con-
> formed to the image of his Son, that he should be the
> firstborn among many brethren. And those whom he
> has predestined, them he has also called; and those
> whom he has called, them he has also justified, and
> those whom he has justified, them he has glorified.
> What then shall we say to these things? If God is for
> us, who is against us? (Rom. 8:28–31)

Our glory is hidden both from our own and others' eyes, until
we reach heaven. In this we are only like our master who divested
himself of all that was his and took on the nature of a slave,
that he might truly be ours and we his, for all time. His descent
from heaven into matter and back again through the tomb to resurrection, ascension, and glorification in heaven created a great para-
bolic curve by means of which he has offered to us a stairway
into heaven.

But we can ascend this stairway only by means of Christ. He is
the way, and there is no other. "We have to be closely fitted into
the pattern of his resurrection" if we are to go where he is now, but
the only way of reaching this identification in glory is by a previous identification in humiliation, suffering, and death through join-
ing ourselves with him in his passion.

"Do you not know that all we who have been baptized
into Christ Jesus have been baptized into his death? For we were

buried with him by means of baptism into death, in order that, just as Christ has arisen from the dead through the glory of the Father, so we also may walk in newness of life" (Rom. 6:3–4).

The Spiritual Life Must Develop

Baptism initiates a process that must develop and mature through a whole lifetime. There can be nothing static in the spiritual life. There is never a time when we have arrived at where God means us to be, until we have died. However far we go, it is little but a foothill in the Himalayan range of sanctity, and to rest in self-complacency while we admire the precipitous slopes we have conquered is merely to invite the devil to cast such a fog between us and the heights Christ beckons us to that we are likely never to catch a glimpse of them again.

However far one goes, one is still an unprofitable servant, one has done only what one should have done, and less than that—far, far less. And by whose power did one do it anyway? Who is that "elder brother" who went before and cut the footholds in the rock face and left the rope fastened there to guide us? What could there possibly be to congratulate oneself on?

Baptism is only a beginning. The rest is love and effort our whole lifelong. The resurrection was bought by the Passion, and because the mystical body is an actuality, not a metaphor, we, in some mysterious but real way, have to participate in the sufferings of our master. That alone is what gives meaning to the weight of misery on humankind. That alone is what has power to ennoble pain and glorify humiliation and put sweetness into deprivation. The further we let Christ draw us into his Passion the closer we become united with him. The inevitable result is a secret powerhouse of spiritual energy and strength to endure within us and a sense of exalted meaningfulness that makes the unbearable bearable.

Much that is inspiring and helpful has been written about participating with Christ in his Passion, but little (in comparison) has been written about dying and being buried with him and finally being raised up into his risen life. Of course, here on earth, we can never enter fully into his risen life, but all the same it is true that those who submit to the climax of the passion pass through a kind of spiritual death that is followed by entombment and, by the grace of God, may culminate into a glorious resurrection, into a degree of union with Christ that is the highest attainable while in the body.

What other state can truly be implied by the words, "It is now no longer I who live, but Christ lives in me"? The culmination of Christ's life was not his crucifixion but his resurrection and glorification. In his risen state he yet remained upon this earth for forty days. In his glorified state he exists in every soul that is in a state of grace. The culmination of the spiritual life, the peak of loving, lies not in interior crucifixion but in interior resurrection.

He who raised Lazarus from a four-day death is mighty enough to snatch up into the bosom of his glory the soul who is prepared to endure the worst pitch of human suffering and so enter into his entombment with him.

After his crucifixion and death, our Lord was taken down from the cross and shut into a sealed tomb where the mysterious metamorphosis of the resurrection took place—there, in the lonely, silent dark. The soul, journeying into full union with Christ, follows this cycle also. Having freely chosen the way of total renunciation, it enters into a series of annihilations that culminate in an interior crucifixion that is the soul's final capitulation. Here, it seems, God has indeed done his worst, and the climax of anguish is over.

"For I, the Lord your God, am a jealous God." The jealousy of God is fiercer and more possessive than that of the most fanatical of earthly lovers. So that he may possess completely what is the object of his devouring love, he ruthlessly casts out all that could impede his invasion, yet the object of this purging is to make something so beautiful that it will awe even the angels.

Gerard Manley Hopkins cried:

> Wert thou my enemy, O thou my friend,
> How wouldst thou worse, I wonder, than thou dost
> Defeat, thwart me?
> (*Poems of Gerard Manley Hopkins*, 68)

Spiritual Growth and Strife

Here again is one of those curious and painful paradoxes that make up the essential conflict of the spiritual life. Growth is the product of strife, and here the beloved God, the merciful and all-tender, is experienced as the malevolent enemy. To continue to will to affirm his goodness during this trial is one of the severest tests of faith and trust and hope. Of charity too, for the soul must make act after act of love to him who seems only the author of disaster.

Someone has said that Christianity is the worship of a sadist by masochists, and so it may seem to the outsider or even to those who read of intense interior sufferings without having endured them themselves. However, to those who go down into the pit of darkness, the certainty that all this apparent visitation of wrath is, in reality, an aspect of God's most especial love, remains unshaken. Whatever the emotions experience, the will does not waver in its affirmation that God is good and loving and that his terrible tenderness wounds only in order to bestow that bliss which cannot be attained by any other means.

With Job they say, "Slay me though he might, I will wait for him" (Job 13:15). These, of course, were our Lord's dispositions in his Passion, and it is only by means of the graces he won there and shares now with his followers that the soul in travail is able to cling to God in this worst spasm of separation from all worldly and sensible comforts and consolations.

When, at last, the stone is rolled across the mouth of the tomb and all is still, a numb composure takes over. There is a strong feeling that there is nothing more to lose, for it has all been given up or taken away. A curious sense of lightness is combined with an equally curious sense of oppression. The worst is certainly over, but there is to be no resurrection yet.

Instead the soul sojourns in a place between nightfall and dawn, where its very insensibility is a kind of muted anguish. It seems that it is journeying along an endless, dark, confined tunnel, or that it is being stifled in the confinement of the rock tomb. The sense of the heavy hillside pressing in all around results almost in spiritual claustrophobia. One can scarcely breathe or move. It is suffocating. Something is pressing close on every side, but there is no labeling it or grasping it.

This painful pressure causes a kind of dread mingled with intolerable longing. Torn from the soul, over and over, is the cry, "How long, O Lord, how long?"

> Will resurrection morning come? Graveclothes
> and spices veil that mutilated flesh.
> Love made into a Man for us. Conspiring darkness
> of this stony sepulchre curves a sheltering vault
> about the corpse of God.
>   Night-silent are all birds
> and winds make no sound, waiting. Rocks
> are massive sentinels honeycombed with tombs.
> The guards lean on their spears, mistrustful in the mute,
> uncanny vigilance of this garden for the dead.
>   Out of the night I cry unto thee, O Lord,
>   and in the hollow sound shell of my everlasting tomb.
>   I raise my death-stopped voice and sing
>   the canticle of the grave, the song of annihilation.
> Will resurrection morning come? Who could have thought
> such kingly limbs could lie so still! O long
> this vigil to the dawn! World that Word spoke
> strains for the lilt of his stricken tongue,
> yearns, shocked, for the press of his unstirring foot.

No nightingale dare sing. No moon gleams.
Darkness is over the face of the earth—the brooding night
envelops those that slew and those that mourn the slain.
Magdalen lies down in the tent of her hair and weeps.
    Out of the night I cry unto thee, O Lord!
    In the black, bitter salt shrubs of the desert,
    in the cruel eclipse, in the hollow pit of emptiness,
    I will wait for thee, Lord, as thou commandest me.

Will resurrection morning come? Who stirs
in the womb-heavy dimness?
(The root in the deep dungeons of the soil,
the sap in the trunk's secret tunnels, the seed
swelling to life in the grave of last year's mould.)
Death where is your sting? Light levels the dark
like a warrior's shaft, and the soldiers swoon with fear
as the indomitable Word speaks the universe once more.
    In a sleeping land
a gray dawn lips the rim of the world and turns to gold.
Sorrow lasts but a night, and joy has come with the morn.
    Out of the night I cry unto thee, O Lord!
    The terror of the grave surrounds me with dread—
    but you are my help in time of trouble, my rock;
    my soul waits patiently for your perpetual light.
(Dent, "Entombment")

Christ's Apparent Withdrawal From the Soul

Perhaps the cruelest part of this state of entombment is the sense of being unable to reach Christ. The intense personal identification with him that was the soul's during its union with his passion gave everything purpose and meaning. There was no ultimate loneliness because all was endured cleaving to Christ. But now in this tomb, he too is still and silent. There is no response from him. There is no way of getting close to him. The dynamism of spiritual intercommunication seems to have broken down.

The Lord of the universe, the King of the heart, is mute and still. The tomb is indeed the place of nothingness, the crossing out of everything. The soul is buried in darkness with the Lord, and all that takes place now is beyond what can be readily comprehended in the ordinary way. It is rather like the secret growth within a tree during the quiescent winter months. There is no apparent sign of change or renewal, but in the dark, inward places all is being prepared for the epiphany in the spring.

The whole of nature works on the principle of death and renewal. It is similar in the psychological realm. For character and personality to mature and develop, there must be continual change, dying on one level in order to be reborn on another. In the spiritual life it is the same, except that here the soul is dying to the world in order to be reborn into Christ.

Its belief in this life of glory is what sustains it during the dark numbness of entombment. The supernatural virtue of hope infuses an element that is absent from all purely psychological cycles of change and evolution. What is aimed at and hoped for is not of this world and indeed entails total renunciation of all that is created. This is not a striving for "the mature personality," "the good life," "the strong, integrated character," "peace of mind," "psychological balance," or any other of today's handy catch phrases.

Instead it is shooting an arrow right out of this universe into what is quite unattainable by unaided human powers. It is an admission of absolute poverty, an embrace of impotence, a kissing of humiliation. It is a deliberate choice of the lowest place of all, and in the eyes of the worldy-wise, it always seems a kind of contemptible or pitiable madness.

St. Paul, with his unequaled insight into these profound truths of the spiritual life, expresses it in a passage crammed with meaning and full of power:

> Do you not know that all we who have been baptized into Christ Jesus have been baptized into his death? For we were buried with him by means of baptism into

> death, in order that, just as Christ has arisen from the dead through the glory of the Father, so we also may walk in newness of life. For if we have been united with him in the likeness of his death, we shall be so in the likeness of his resurrection also. For we know that our old self has been crucified with him, in order that the body of sin may be destroyed, that we may no longer be slaves to sin; for he who is dead is acquitted of sin. But if we have died with Christ, we believe that we shall also live together with Christ; for we know that Christ, having risen from the dead, dies now no more, death shall no longer have dominion over him. For the death that he died, he died to sin once for all, but the life that he lives, he lives unto God. Thus do you consider yourselves also as dead to sin, but alive to God in Christ Jesus. (Rom. 6:3–11)

It appears that the soul has died and been buried with Christ; yet, powerful though this impression is and true though it is in one sense, in another it is an illusion. It is an illusion because there is only one thing that can cause real death in the soul, and that is grave sin. As long as it remains in a state of grace, the baptized soul is alive with the life of God, possessing the Blessed Trinity.

An Opportunity for Expiation

Perhaps an analogy can be drawn with Christ when he who had no sin was yet "made sin" for us.

This entombment of the soul that is in a state of grace and this subjective experiencing of death and annihilation is part of the suffering of the just for the unjust. By patiently enduring this grievous trial and ever continuing to exercise the theological virtues, the soul may, as it were, take the place of guilty souls before God, making expiation for them and winning the graces of repentance and reconciliation with God for those who truly are in the death of mortal sin.

Added to this is the chance to make expiation for personal past sins and also to enter into a full realization of the actual sinful state that every human soul would possess were it not for the grace of God. Stripped of his grace, even the greatest saints would become cesspools of corruption.

In the tomb the soul has the chance to experience this truth powerfully and subjectively. It is like Lazarus, whose body after four days made the air foul with its corruption, and yet Christ could and did say, "Lazarus, come forth," and he came out not only living, but whole.

In the tomb God leaves the soul to itself to experience its own foulness and impotence and to learn humility in numbness. Yet all the while it is not dead, but living. "Why do you seek the living one among the dead? He is not here, but has risen.... He goes before you into Galilee" (Luke 24:5; Mark 16:7).

Faith, in the midst of subjective entombment, is in the risen Lord. Hope is in being raised up, as Lazarus was, to join that risen life, a life "that looks toward God," the life of the free soul. "But now set free from sin and become slaves to God, you have your fruit unto sanctification, and as your end, life everlasting.... You also, through the body of Christ, have been made to die to the Law, so as to belong to another who has risen from the dead, in order that we may bring forth fruit unto God" (Rom. 6:22; 7:4).

It is the risen Lord who permeates the whole of creation, in and through whom the soul released from the bondage to sin will achieve its glorification. From heaven the risen Lord pours out his life into the veins and least capillaries of his mystical body. "We have faith to believe that we shall share his life," and we shall share it not only after death in heaven but by slowly increasing degrees in this life, as we surrender ourselves to him.

The tomb is the grave of self-love and self-will. Here our true life becomes the life that is hidden away with Christ in God, a life in which numberless, small, hidden acts of love propel the soul closer and closer to God.

Continually the risen Lord is calling to the soul, "Come forth!" and yet it is powerless to move until he himself has transformed the grave clothes of its natural self with the shining garment of his grace. None may come to the wedding feast without this garment, though all be invited, and it is a garment that only God can give in the perfection that merits complete union with him.

The life of the tomb, then, is the life of faith, hope, and charity—of trust, patience, and humility. It is true that the risen Lord permeates the whole of the universe, but he cannot be subjectively experienced by, and united with, the soul until it is pure. "Blessed are the clean of heart, for they shall see God" (Matt. 5:8).

To long for him and for him only is the soul's response to his "drawing," and when this longing is perfectly single-minded, then he will manifest himself in the dwelling place he has prepared for himself.

In the meantime, the years of waiting and longing can be compared with the sojourn of the Israelites in the desert. The promised land is real and there. God is true to his promise and guides us in the pillar of fire and cloud, but only those who are faithful will reach the goal.

The whole process is part of the action of God's love. Because of the impurities within us, because of psychological twists, because of emotional attachments to created things, we experience his action as a fiery torment, an annihilating darkness. But this cannot alter the fact that it is love, and the more we abandon ourselves to its force and demands, the more quickly we shall enter into the promised land, which for Christians is union with the risen Lord.

But in all these things we overcome because of him who has loved us. For I am sure that neither death, nor life, nor angels, nor principalities, nor things present, nor things to come, nor powers, nor height, nor depth, nor any other creature will be able to separate us from the love of God, which is in Christ Jesus our Lord. (Rom. 8:37–39)

[Untitled]

In the stillness of eternity I rest in you;
in the silence of infinity I drink your love.
There is no place to designate for the place is everywhere,
there is no time to pinpoint for this is the everlasting eternal now.
It lolls upon the horizon, neither waxing nor waning,
just being there to remind me time is sliding into eternity.
It sheds an effulgence, soft yet indestructible,
and deep within it, you, its source, rest,
            waiting for the chosen moment,
the time of coming forth, annunciation's fruit,
            mission completed.

Now is the time for being there patiently—a difficult task
but one that hones the heart and readies it for battle
with itself. Strangely detached, I keep vigil for the outcome—
involved, yet only an attentive watcher, keeping score.
How is one to decide? Mostly, it is impossible, the balance
sways from side to side, and what is loss is gain,
and what is gain is loss. Best to leave it all to the grey
            and wizened scorekeeper
whose centuries of practice have made him accurate
to penetrate disguise and uncover the secret lurking within.

The Night of Faith

Cross and Crown (September 1976)

Alone, my first time in London—so much was overwhelming and confusing to me, a fifty-five-year-old New Zealander. For example, I was baffled for a fortnight or more by the subway system. I was unable meaningfully—to use the "in" word—to link up the Transport Authority's diagramatic map with reality. Since the entire population of New Zealand would take up only one-third of Greater London, the larger stations seemed to me designed to reduce any newcomer to impotence and nearly to despair. I had never before seen so many escalators, stairs, tunnels, passages, platforms, all variously labeled and generously supplied with busy, preoccupied people hurrying along, knowing where they were going. Finally, after weeks of frustrating wrong turns in this maze, illumination suddenly came and I found the right path. I "saw" and understood.

This experience was curiously like that intuitive, spiritual illumination that in a flash bestows tremendously important insights upon one's love and service of God. The interior life, like the subway system in London or any other large city, has a pattern and a purpose, and one enters it intending to get to a particular destination as expeditiously and as directly as possible. The maps and diagrams supplied by the Transport Authority are the Church's guidelines of how to serve God and neighbor—to do this, refrain from that, avoid dangerous situations, and forge ahead toward union with God. These directives may not be as clear-cut and explicit as they used to be, but they are still available for newcomers and proficients alike.

Proficiency and confidence come through practice. Faults are overcome by persistent effort, deliberate sin is avoided by training and discipline, and habits of virtue are established that make the spiritual life seem almost effortless. The traveler knows exactly where he is going and moves confidently and efficiently from train to train, to get there perhaps even sooner than he expected.

Then comes the equivalent of derailment or power failure. All maps, diagrams, directions, labels, and guidebooks that could be utilized smoothly and efficiently are useless, quite meaningless no matter how much intelligence and expertise can be mustered. There is nothing at all left to see, read, hold, grasp, refer to, or rely on. The subway system still exists, but for the moment there is no way to perceive the signs or cope with tunnels, stairways, platforms, entrances, and exits. There is no recognizable way to reach the ultimate destination—God. This traumatic condition is called the night of faith. Both nouns here are important, for without faith the night can cause severe psychological disturbances and even breakdowns when one enters into or remains for extended periods of time in this state.

Natural Aids Removed

In essence, God has removed all human, natural aids in order to guide the traveler through infused faith, hope, and love. The predominantly active role is now a passive one. Reliable methods and systems must be unlearned for one to become completely pliant and receptive to whatever the Spirit chooses as the method and system (or rather, nonmethod and nonsystem) most suitable for a particular stage and time.

The traveler feels trapped in darkness, while it may be as noon for someone else. "Dark, dark, dark! Irremediably dark amid the blaze of noon!" The blessed state of light and confidence is no more, and the traveler feels that God has destined him to remain blind and lost forever. He is as it were in a state of purgatory in this life.

He can do little or nothing to help himself. Trying to act bravely and strike out on one's own initiative leads only to disaster. The firmly established habits of virtue are one's only salvation.

People do not die in the night of faith. Although they do not realize it (if they did, they would not be living by faith), they are coming more and more alive. They are being taught to live with that everlasting life that Jesus brought through the incarnation. But because this is so different from their ordinary experience, they feel completely lost. Paradoxically, they are becoming active participators through their passivity in the extended incarnation through which the Redeemer continues his saving work in time and space.

When most convinced of failure and ineptitude, one is closest to fulfilling God's purpose. When one has no idea of what he ought to do or know and in desperation blindly follows some obscure prompting from deep within himself, he is most likely on the right platform and boarding the proper train to take him to God.

The Spirit Purposefully Active

The Christian believes, against all evidence to the contrary, that the Spirit is purposefully active in his life. Rather than set certain self-chosen goals and plan directions to travel, he learns to be passive to what often seem to be the quixotic, absurd vagaries of fate. By removing all signs and guidelines, God shows that faith is the way of unknowing, undoing, unpossessing, and unsureness. One cannot rely on himself or any other human being, but only on the Trinity at work in a hidden manner beyond understanding.

One must learn to be a failure so that God may be glorified. One must learn to change direction without the comfort of explanations and reassurances, to go the same route over and over in idiotic repetition, apparently getting nowhere at all and being content about it. This is humiliating and is meant to be just that. Whatever degree of human cleverness one possesses, however extensive one's human knowledge is, it is very little or no help and can indeed be a positive hindrance when it puts itself in the way of God's action or direction.

The one experiencing the night of faith tries to explain, but becomes inarticulate: "I want to try to explain.... I mean I think it's this way...no, that's wrong.... You see, it began when I.... No, it didn't. I can't remember."

Others who do not have the problem or do not comprehend it merely ask, "What on earth are you talking about? All the maps and signs are still there. I can see them myself. Have you gone blind or something?"

God Drawing Closer

All this happens because God is truly beyond human understanding, and this incomprehensible One is drawing closer during the night of faith. God is not known in any intellectual sense, but experienced directly as one opens more to him, permitting him to enter deeper and to manage one's life more fully for him. The humiliation of impotence and confusion, the stupidity of feeling ignorant and lost, reduces one to docility beneath the Spirit's inspirations and actions. One becomes content, as humiliation deepens, to be nothing but the recipient of whatever graces God chooses to bestow and, more, to remain unaware of being a recipient.

Well-developed virtues for one entering the night of faith are just as important as well-developed muscles for a star athlete. From a moment when one can say with a cheerful wave in passing, "I'm getting on fine, Lord. Thanks for the help. I'll let you know when I need you," one comes to a realization that he needs the Lord every moment, every step, and every turn. Mysteriously, painfully, humiliatingly, longingly, and self-effacingly, one learns that without God one is nothing, that God's ways are not one's own ways, that the last shall be first and the first last. When God takes over the subway, human timetables have no validity or use. In faith, the Spirit trains one to travel the subway when all directional aids have been removed.

Summons

All right—I'm coming. Don't pester me.
It was you who set me off upon this journey
with all its problematical twists and turns
and no map—so you must realize
the difficulties and the inevitable delays.
I've done my best. I'm different from you
(and yet the same, being derivative)
I can't just think it—and be there. I must
pick and choose my route to suit your whims
not mine. The reasons for your whims
are usually obscure and in a foreign tongue
but I do my best to transcribe. I can't help it
if I get you wrong. Sometimes I find it hard
not to believe you tangle me up on purpose
like a boy with an insect crawling on his shoe—
sometimes just observed, at others teased,
and in the end just squashed from boredom.

All right—I'm coming. Give me time.
One day I'll know what you intend
then nothing and no one will impede
my headlong progress. I'll fling myself
into your widespread arms
and rest my head against your mighty heart
and cry, "I'm home! I've come home at last!
I'm safe for all eternity. I've arrived!"

Dark Nights and Shining Ones

New Zealandia (date unknown)

This year is St. John of the Cross's fourth centenary. He was born near Avila in Spain in 1542 and died on 14 December 1591, in Ubeda, Spain. On 26 December 1726, he was canonized by Benedict XIII and declared a Doctor of the Church by Pius XI on 24 August 1926.

Though John is known and revered by most Carmelites as one of their own holiest friars and greatest teachers on the spiritual life and prayer, lay Catholics, if they have heard of him at all, tend to have only hazy notions of who he was and even hazier ones of his teachings. Yet there are undoubtedly many simple, holy, inconspicuous, utterly dedicated lovers of God, in both the lay and religious states, who have passed through at least some of the spiritual journey that he dissects and explains in such a masterly way. There will even be some who have attained the due end of those purifications and trials and have entered permanently into what Scripture calls "being filled with the fullness of God" (Eph. 3:19) and "the perfect goodness in us for the glory and praise of God" (Phil. 1:11).

Jesus came that we might "have life and have it more abundantly" (John 10:10). All John of the Cross's writings elaborate on the basic teachings of Jesus and the pointers to them throughout the Old Testament. He demonstrates convincingly how those who are prepared to give all as Jesus gave and gives all to us will

121

enter even in this life "the kingdom of Heaven within" and "the peace of God that passes all understanding."

The arduous journey toward this state is described in the two treatises—*The Ascent of Mount Carmel* and *The Dark Night of the Soul*. Both John of the Cross and Teresa of Avila (who were closely associated) call its final consummation "transforming union" or "spiritual marriage," the latter generally referring to the discernible graces, and the former to the indiscernible, basic spiritual state that transforms one's whole being and life in an undramatic but fundamental way. Baptism initiates all Christians into union with the Trinity "in the name of the Father, and of the Son, and of the Holy Spirit"—John shows how this union is brought to glorious fruition.

"Shining ones" in the title of this essay refers to this state of being where we are filled with the glory of God, even while we continue on this earth in the dark night of faith—but in its positive, not negative mode.

St. John of the Cross's treatises are not easy reading nowadays, because the scholastic wording used belongs to a past age and because John was a graduate and teacher of theology. Yet it is possible to understand and personally apply his doctrines. People, and not only religious, have done so ever since they became available, and the term "the dark night" has passed into common usage, though not always correctly understood.

They demonstrate that we do not have to wait till heaven to be exalted in the Lord. Purgatory can be endured and emerged from in this life, and we can begin our heaven here on earth.

Most who have heard of St. John of the Cross link him with the term "the dark night of the soul," and rightly so, for it is his teachings about the spiritual "nights" that will be of interest to most. His other two treatises, *The Spiritual Canticle* and *The Living Flame of Love* are for the saints—but also for those who have fallen in love with God in this life, yearn to be made one with him, and are prepared to drink Jesus' cup with him. What John writes (from his personal experience) of that "flame of love" and its fruit of "spiritual marriage" will inspire them to do and suffer anything in order to be snatched up by the Spirit into that blessed, blissful state of being.

But it is his exposition of the dark night that will help them understand and persevere through the purifications that must be endured before we can enter into the fullness of union, whether on earth or in heaven.

John of the Cross is not easy reading, but his treatises on the nature and consequences of the living presence of God in us are among the most profound and psychologically exact and perceptive of all those made by the spiritual masters of the Church. Everything he wrote was based on the foundation stones of his own experience of all the stages of purification up to the final blessedness of full union, enriched by his practical knowledge gained in directing many others traveling the same route. Also involved were his extensive theological knowledge and his love of and familiarity with Scripture. Since he was also a poet, he was clever at using comparisons and making clear, profound spiritual truths by metaphor and analogy.

First we must understand that John speaks of our whole purposeful progress toward union as "night," because it has to be made in the "darkness of faith" since, however full our union with God is in this life, it will never include the face-to-face beatific vision of heaven.

In *The Ascent of Mount Carmel*, he explains, "In the night of the sense there still remains some light, for the understanding and reason remain, and are not blinded. But this spiritual night, which is faith, deprives the soul of everything, both as to the understanding and as to sense.... The less the soul works with its own ability, the more securely it journeys, because it journeys more in faith"

(*Ascent* 2:1:3). It is necessary to realize that he is here referring mainly to the transition from meditative prayer to contemplation proper, for the darkness to the intellect that is faith "tells us of things which we have never seen or understood" (i.e., that which is divine), "nor have we seen or understood aught that resembles them, since there is naught that resembles them at all" (*Ascent* 2:3:3).

In the dark night it seems we are being turned into spiritual "zombies," while we remain quite capable of functioning normally with everyday life and its duties and concerns.

In *The Ascent of Mount Carmel* and *The Dark Night of the Soul*, John sets out to trace the whole pilgrim journey from an unredeemed state of immersion in sin and alienation from God through the various purifications necessary to the highest level of union with Perfect Love possible in this life. He systematically divides the stages of this exposition into the active and passive nights of both sense and spirit.

During these we are progressively detached by grace and work at detaching ourselves from what is alien to God so as to become partially, and at last wholly, attached to and at one with him. All the way we must cleave to his will rather than to our own and travel in faith, hope, and love as gifts of the Spirit help to reorientate us. Any committed Christian who is sincere and consistent inevitably travels some of this route, whatever terminology is used. Usually it is the earlier part of *The Ascent of Mount Carmel,* which includes renouncing grave sins and struggling against lesser ones and sinful tendencies in general. It is a process of striving, falling, getting up, and going on, with a generous lacing of worldly pursuits and distractions, and a good dose of self-indulgence and wilfulness.

In *The Ascent of Mount Carmel,* we do what we can, with carrying degrees of sincerity and perseverance, and God gives us grace to help us along and strengthen our resolve. John explains he is not "treating of the *lack* of things" when he stresses how necessary are detachment and quietening of all desires except that for union with God, but rather he is "treating of the detachment from them of the taste and desire, for it is this that leaves the soul free and void of them, although it may have them" (*Ascent* 3:4). It is so very difficult for the "rich man to enter the kingdom of heaven" (which is within) because of the strong inner attachment of his will and heart to his riches—whether material or spiritual. (John of the Cross is masterly at exposing the nature of attachment to spiritual riches and the way we pride ourselves on them as if we had made them for ourselves instead of receiving them free from the Spirit.) Our hearts are centered on them, not on God, no matter how punctilious our outward observance of our religion may be. But it is the inner person that must be renewed through *metanoia,* as our renewal programs stress.

John works out minutely through the three books of *The Ascent of Mount Carmel* what has to be renounced to make room for God and how we go about it, working inward until he reaches the deeper realm of the spirit—even what today we would call the subconscious and unconscious. "The truth is that the will must never rejoice save only in that which is to the honor and glory of God" (*Ascent* 3:18). Only then can Christ "come unto his own" and be received royally.

It is a long haul, and at a certain stage we seem to have come to a full stop.

This is because we are being called to enter, or rather let happen to us, the dark night of the soul, where we are not so much actively doing and renouncing, as passively opening ourselves wide enough to grace and the Spirit's action so as to let God work in us to achieve what is beyond our own powers.

However, as in most inner states of being, all the purgations, active and passive, of sense and of spirit, interpenetrate and interconnect. Therefore the books of *The Ascent of Mount Carmel* and *The Dark Night of the Soul* need to be absorbed as a whole and understood as one mighty act of spiritual reintegration to enable us to become fully identified with Christ.

John gives various signs by which entry into the night is normally initiated by the Spirit. These are persistent aridity and inability to pray as one has been accustomed, coupled with the effort to keep the prayer time as usual; deliberate sin is no longer committed and the person has long been dedicated to doing and suffering God's will; one is more aware of the painful absence of God than of his consoling presence, and this causes anxiety about possible personal failure and fear of backsliding. No cause for the state can be found through ill-health or lukewarmness in doing one's duty and practicing the virtues, especially kindness.

There are definite, recognized causes for the above. The prime one is that God is now leading us into a deeper kind of prayer, simpler, less definable, more passive and receptive than active, and self-regulated. Contemplation is beginning to happen in us (just when it seems nothing at all is ever happening) as a gift from the Spirit in a wrapping quite strange to us. We are learning to stay still and submit, "for contemplation is naught else than a secret, peaceful and loving infusion from God, which, if it be permitted, enkindles the soul with the spirit of love" (*Dark Night* 1:10:6).

Just as painful and even alarming is the dread that God has ceased to cherish us, and we to love him, because we can no longer feel warm and positive in our relationship with him. In fact, we are being cleansed through this numbness of the impurities of self-seeking and even spiritual gluttony that make us seek God more for what he gives us in emotional fulfillments of various kinds, than out of a longing to serve and love him, no matter what. He is now teaching us to love and serve even more committedly, though he seems never to look our way. Warm emotions are giving way to bare faith that he is there, he *does* love, he *never* will spurn or betray, he is *always* to be trusted. This is the night of sense.

> The night which we have called that of sense may
> and should be called a kind of correction and restraint
> of the desire rather than purgation. The reason is that
> all the imperfections and disorders of the sensual part

have their strength and root in the spirit, where all
habits, both good and bad, are brought into subjection,
and thus, until these are purged, the rebellions and
depravities of sense cannot be purged thoroughly.
(*Dark Night* 2:3:1)

The more we deliberately practice such denuded love, the deeper
it becomes and the closer we approach to God in the darkness, even
while we feel there is neither love nor closeness.

In this early part of the night it is more or less the surface elements of the psyche that are being purified. Later, if we persevere,
we will come to the passive night of the spirit, which is the most
profound purification possible and is the equivalent of purgatory
in this life. John of the Cross says many enter the dark night of
sense, the early one, but few the night of the spirit. Those who do,
and emerge from it in this life, are the saints, whether canonized
or unknown and unsung in this life.

An extremely important virtue to be consistently practised in
the dark night is perseverance. There is a real temptation to give
up and smother one's pain and loneliness for God in distractions
and pleasures of various kinds.

Many turn back at this stage, and so sink into mediocrity with
the danger of lapsing completely. This is one main reason why a
knowledgeable, gentle, kind but firm director is almost an essential both in the early stages of the dark night and later through the
passive night of the spirit.

The wrong kind of guide can do grave harm, and John of the
Cross inveighs passionately against these and their characteristics
in *The Living Flame of Love* (3:41–62). He calls them "blind
guides" and urges them to "remember that the principal agent and
guide, and mover of souls is not the director, but the Holy Spirit,"
and that "they themselves are only instruments to lead souls in the
way of perfection by the faith and the law of God, according to the
spirit God is giving each one" (3:46).

One of the main roles of the director is to give reassurance that "all is well" when what we are experiencing suggests that nothing is "well." The dark night of the soul is a severe testing of love as well as of faith, for the Spirit's work of purification, especially as it sinks deeper in, is exceedingly painful, though the degree of suffering and penetration of grace are in exact proportion to the degree of union with the Trinity that God ordains for this person. Those called higher find the climb gets more and more arduous and demanding, as any ascender of Mt. Everest will confirm. We are likely to think wistfully of St. Thérèse's spiritual "elevator" that she devised to take her straight up to Jesus—but it is a fact that, if we practise her humility, childlike trust, and perfect abandonment, we shall both be invited and be able to enter it with her.

Like St. Paul, John of the Cross "proclaims a message of wisdom to those who are spiritually mature,...[it is] God's secret wisdom.... As Scripture says, 'What no one ever saw or heard, what no one ever thought could happen, is the very thing God prepared for those who love him'" (1 Cor. 2:6, 9).

As we are drawn more deeply into the passive night of the spirit, we experience what John calls "enkindlings" and enlarges on in *The Living Flame of Love* and *The Spiritual Canticle.* In *The Dark Night of the Soul,* he explains that there occurs, as a brief illumination of the deepest, darkest suffering of this night, "an enkindling of spiritual love in the soul, which, in the midst of these dark confines, feels itself to be keenly and sharply wounded in strong divine love, and to have a certain realization and foretaste of God" (*Dark Night* 2:11:1). Such brief respites of consummated, mutual love bring new courage to endure and perseverance in practicing faith, hope, and love. They are a foretaste of the "shining night" to come.

But before the supreme grace of this uninterrupted blessedness is attained, the soul must be "reformed, ordered and tranquilized" into "the state of innocence that was Adam's" (*Dark Night* 2:24:2).

At last we put first things first without a fierce struggle against base, self-seeking urges, desires, and motives. At last we understand what loving and being loved are all about, as God draws us deeper into "a new bond of loving possession" in which we are given "substantial" (i.e., in our deepest levels of being) "touches of Divine union" (*Dark Night* 2:24:3).

The effect is total concentration of our heart and will upon God and his will and the longing to be a channel of his love for others, together with the assurance that we are. "The soul sees naught, neither looks at aught, neither stays in aught that is not God" (*Dark Night* 2:25:3) and is about to be drawn into full union.

The Dark Night of the Soul treatise breaks off abruptly at this threshold of unadulterated spiritual fulfillment, but John deals extensively with its bliss in the other two treatises, *The Living Flame of Love* and *The Spiritual Canticle*.

It is impossible to give anything more than an outline of John of the Cross's teachings in a brief article. He is by no means "out of date" because he lived and wrote in the sixteenth century and we are in the twentieth. His doctrines are timeless and of particular significance to those who love and long for holiness in order to glorify God and serve their neighbor in selfless love and joy.

Instrument

Wind, pneuma, restless one—you do not cease
until your work is done. A busy housewife
comes to mind—but you are far more thorough,
concentrating on those crevices, corners
and slits where cobwebs and wetas
lurk in dark reclusion.

Like that mighty wind coming at Pentecost
to fill the house with bustle and commotion—
you descended upon us, rose from our secret fastnesses
and took possession as of right of every room and corridor.

This is the way you prefer to work, channeling away
where rudimentary pathways have been cleared.
The debris and the rubbish piles, the broken tools
and pieces chosen with such care yet now discarded
litter the paths we try out one by one until our feet
sense familiar ground.

Our pace is quickened—
eagerness of journey's end in sight inspires and invigorates.

The Log of Wood

Mount Carmel (Spring 1984)

In St. John of the Cross's treatise on interior purgation, book 2 of *The Dark Night of the Soul* deals with the ultimate purgations, the passive ones of the spirit. In these it is as if a series of depth charges are let off in the furthest levels of the psyche, and the resultant debris and artifacts hurled to the surface and into consciousness are dealt with by the Holy Spirit for our sanctification.

This, the deepest purgation possible in this life, is purgatory here on earth. Those who pass through it before death go straight to God at death. They have been elevated into transforming union and have "become Christ." They live, but not of themselves, for Christ is the life principle in them, and by their own choice they are controlled and impelled by the Trinity.

The purposes of these deeper, passive purgations are many. They lead us to face the truth about ourselves and accept it. The result is what Jung calls "individuation," the incorporation into the conscious self of the iniquitous "shadow" lurking within from which we like to hide, or whose existence we deny.

The action of the Holy Spirit reveals the deepest, most hidden roots (i.e., the unconscious origins) of the behavior patterns, complexes, obsessions, and compulsions that rule us. They also bring to light the rationalizations by means of which we excuse ourselves while we manipulate and use others for our own honor and glory, not God's, ascribing to ourselves altruistic motives and the highest ideals.

Also revealed are power mechanisms that run smoothly on the oil of our lust for recognition and aggrandizement; the fleshly appetites that have us in their grip and that our will cannot control, so that we assure ourselves that their satisfaction is essential to our spiritual development; our pitiful, infantile cravings that we have never outgrown, because we never received perfect nurturing from our parents, since they were afflicted and warped by original sin just as we are.

These and all other imperfections and evils rooted in us have to be exposed, faced, and come to terms with before we can receive the fullness of divine love and be transformed into Christ.

Chapter 10 of book 2 summarizes the preceding nine chapters' comments on the opening phrase of John's poem, "On A Dark Night." Therefore it is a useful one both to peruse and to meditate upon.

To illustrate his theme the author uses the analogy between the soul being purged and a log of wood slowly being penetrated by fire until it becomes fire itself.

The soul (the log), once completely permeated by divine life (the fire), enters the divine state of transforming union or spiritual marriage (log and fire become one, and the log takes on the properties of fire). This state is what God intends as the destiny and final end of every human being, yet most Christians regard it (if they even realize its existence) as some incredible condition to be found only in canonized saints. They do not link it up with contemporary emphasis on "inner renewal," nor realize that John's teaching is applicable to themselves as they strive to be Christ in and for the modern world.

Admittedly, his terminology, mixed metaphors, and philosophical complexities are formidable—but they are not insurmountable once his key ideas are grasped, and one can see how they relate to oneself struggling to be a better person and to love others for God's sake.

In the passive purgations, the Holy Spirit acts and we remain pliable, receptive, trusting, and cooperative. Our role is to endure and "to let it happen." Not as easy as it sounds, for if we resist we either stop the divine action and so opt for mediocrity or else we make it harder for ourselves by forcing God to take us by storm. Yet it is difficult not to try to repel what is an exceedingly painful process.

Relaxation is the recipe needed—to lie in God's divine providence, as it works on and shapes us, as unresistingly as the log of wood lies in the fire and lets itself be burned. "The divine fire of contemplative love" that purifies us is itself completely holy, pure, benign, and beautiful, while we are possessed by "evil and vicious humors which the soul has never perceived because they have been so deeply rooted and grounded in it; it has never realized, in fact, that it has had so much evil within itself"(*Dark Night* 2:10:2).

These "humors" are what we would now name as the various psychological aberrations and vicious or comparatively harmless tendencies that have been shaping our motives, attitudes, and conduct in ways that we have not realized. They have whipped up prejudices and misplaced ardors, while corrupting all our human relationships with various hard-to-define but certainly evil influences of self-love and self-will.

To see all this, even though only out of the corner of one's eye, as it were, is a serious shock. We are lucky if we have an understanding, wise confessor or director. If not, we have to apply an extra degree of trust and self-abandonment to divine providence and accept the Holy Spirit as our guide. He will certainly perform his role more than adequately if we do not close ourselves off from him and retire into a welter of distractions and activities.

Although we usually remain rational enough to see that these "evil and vicious humors," plus their effects, are not sins as such, to recognize and accept their presence in ourselves constitutes a moral shock. We are not deliberately sinning. In fact, after years of struggle and mortification, deliberate sin has been excised from our lives. Yet, there, deep in us, is revealed "sin" itself. What we see, of course, is original sin and its consequence, concupiscence. "As [the soul] sees in itself that which it saw not before, it is clear to it that not only is it unfit to be seen by God, but deserves his abhorrence, and that he does indeed abhor it" (*Dark Night* 2:10:2).

Of course, God continues to love us in spite of, and even because of everything. What we experience is the impossibility of absolute purity, beauty, and holiness merging with or even touching impurity, ugliness, and evil. As John emphasizes, "two contrarities" cannot mix and merge. This is the state of the log of wood at the beginning, when it is first cast into the fire and the fire's effect is to make it seem even blacker, darker, and dirtier in contrast to its own glorious incandescence. The log has not yet caught fire. It is first blackened by smoke and heat and then has to be dried out before it will burn.

John calls the fire various things: purgative and loving knowledge, divine light, mystical theology, divine fire of contemplative love, loving wisdom, divine purgation, and dark light of divine contemplation.

These titles taken together clearly convey that this purgative activity comes from and is controlled by God. It is mystical and contemplative, being a grace received directly from God, by means of which knowledge of how we appear in his sight is infused into us. This wisdom is not something we could ever reach by natural reason or even the deepest ponderings. It has to be given. It can be given only to those who are receptive.

Humble receptivity coupled with a consuming hunger to be one with the divine are absolute prerequisites for the infusion of these graces.

Having made his analogy, John develops it throughout the rest of this chapter in a brief exposition of each of seven major points.

(1) The fire of God's purgative love that reveals, excises, and disposes of those evil roots underlying our surface behavior is felt by us as painful and destructive. Yet it is the same love that we shall later experience as "light" and as "loving wisdom," permeating us with the tenderest, most solicitous care once it has annihilated our dross.

(2) We feel that God, or Wisdom, is punishing and repelling us. This of course cannot be true, since God is love and his only action is one of infinite, eternal love. What we are, in fact, experiencing is the affliction of seeing ourselves exactly as we are in all our misery, weakness, and wickedness. We had probably assessed ourselves as having reached a reasonable degree of sanctity. It is highly unpleasant to become aware that we have scarcely begun on the purgative way, and it is only human to transfer the blame onto God rather than accept it ourselves.

After all, the human race began doing this in Eden and has gone on ever since compulsively deflecting blame either onto God or someone else—anyone and anywhere as long as I can continue to view myself as praiseworthy and in the right.

This struggle to face up to one's real self has to take place, and the blame has to be accepted and absorbed before we can begin to be sure from experience that the purgative fire is one of "divine light, sweetness and delight" (*Dark Night* 2:10:4). In the meantime, it remains "afflictive." The soul is dark and troubled just as the unlit log of wood until it is dried out and so prepared to receive the flame.

(3) These afflictions are the same as those suffered in purgatory. It is fire that is commonly referred to in describing the sufferings of both purgatory and hell, the only difference between the two states being that one will be terminated and the other is everlasting. (It is part of John's genius in describing the spiritual

life that he uses the metaphor of fire for both the purgative process and the state of transforming union in "the living flame of love.") Often the impression is given that the fire expresses God's revenge, hatred, rejection, and repugnance—all these being vindictively directed toward the sinner.

Old-style mission preachers would revel in descriptions of appalling torments, physical and spiritual, that left no doubt that God was a kind of sadistic torturer. Nuns and brothers used alleviated versions to control naughty children in the classroom, permanently damaging their psyches and their relationship with God in the process. That was the fashion. But it was theologically inexact.

The fire, whether directed on the soul of a saint on earth or in heaven or that of a sinner on earth, in purgatory, or in hell remains the fire of God's love. It causes suffering when there is sin present, only because of the colliding impact between the contraries of God's perfections and our imperfections. The big bang occurs in our psyches with resultant shock waves and even cataclysmic earthquakes.

"For the fire would have no power over them, even though they came into contact with it, if they had no imperfections for which to suffer" (*Dark Night* 2:10:5). God is never anything but perfect, everlasting love. He confronts sin with love, and sin, realizing at last its own nature, recoils in horror. In purgatory it offers itself to God to be cleansed, no matter how much it hurts, and eventually the hurt fades away into bliss. In hell it continues to shriek, "I will not serve!" and the hurt remains permanently. "When the imperfections are consumed, the affliction of the soul ceases and its fruition remains" (2:10:5). The fruition, of course, is union in transforming love with the Trinity.

(4) While the purification is taking effect, love grows more and more insistent in us, as God pours his largesse into the spaces cleared by his own grace for his entry.

"Enkindling of love" is a phrase John often uses in relation to the infusion of grace into the soul. It vividly recalls the image of the log of wood, now lit up and beginning to flame. Once God begins to draw us into the union of love, the enkindling process of his love goes on uninterruptedly, providing we do not deliberately sin. However, we do not necessarily feel any delight or warmth in love, for the reality of grace's presence and influence may well be concealed by the pain of the "dark contemplation" assailing us with that other truth about our helplessness and sinfulness.

When he judges it necessary for our encouragement or right for the just balancing of truths, the Spirit reveals "the work that is being wrought in [the soul]" (*Dark Night* 2:10:6) in its positive, consoling aspect. It is almost as if God takes from the furnace the iron he is working on to give us a chance to have a look and see that change has indeed taken place.

"There is a season for everything, a time for every occupation under heaven: a time for giving birth, a time for dying; a time for planting, a time for uprooting what has been planted; a time for killing, a time for healing; a time for knocking down, a time for building" (Eccles. 3:1–3). The Spirit alone can perfectly assess which season it is with us and which is the appropriate activity. He is to be trusted and obeyed. We face and accept what is revealed to us whether it is shameful or consoling.

(5) The pattern of purgation is cyclical. "After each of these periods of relief the soul suffers once again, more intensely and keenly than before" (*Dark Night* 2:10:7). All the time the flame is penetrating further into the log. This represents God's purgative action striking deeper in us around our roots, so that we may be "purified more inwardly" in a manner "more intimate, subtle, and spiritual" (2:10:7).

What is "intimate" is related to our deepest and most private secrets and concerns. An "intimate" friend knows us very well indeed, receives all our confidences, and takes a personal, searching interest in our lives and our way of living them. What is "subtle" is delicate, precise, dealing in the finer points, able to discern and differentiate accurately, perceptive in a piercing yet considerate manner, having discretion and sensitivity so that it can take all things into consideration while keeping them in perfect balance.

What is "spiritual" has to do with that immortal part of us that survives death and enters eternity. Obviously, it is enduring and crucial in importance in a way that what has to do with the senses and emotions cannot be.

Book 2 of *The Dark Night* has to do with the purifying of this spiritual aspect of our beings. It is a far more refined, penetrating work than that of the purgation of the senses. It is also a much more secret one.

The finesse required is possessed only by the Holy Spirit himself who "reaches the depths of everything, even the depths of God.... Now instead of the spirit of the world, we have received the Spirit that comes from God, to teach us to understand the gifts that he has given us" (1 Cor. 2:11–12). The fire is now refining those "spiritual imperfections ...which are most deeply rooted in [our] inmost parts" (*Dark Night* 2:10:7). In order to accomplish and complete its work it "acts with more force and vehemence in preparing [this] most inward part to possess it" (2:10:7).

The more forceful and even violent a penetration is, the more what is being penetrated is likely to be broken to bits unless it relaxes and submits completely. Perhaps John Donne had in mind the Spirit's "force and vehemence" acting to repel sin, when in his Holy Sonnet XIV he implored God to "Batter my heart...and bend/ Your force, to break, blow, burn and make me new."

Donne accurately understood the need for inner renewal of a radical kind and for purgatory endured, if not in this life, then after it, before God could be encountered. He concludes this powerful sonnet, in which he encapsulates so much truth in metaphors of capture, by the startling paradox: "Take me to you, imprison me, for I / Except you enthrall me, never shall be free, / Nor ever chast, except you ravish me."

The idea of being ravished by the Holy Spirit; i.e., being penetrated to one's "most inward [spiritual] part to possess it," horrifies and frightens the lukewarm and mediocre. To the ardent lover of God, who hungers and thirsts for him day and night, it is a call to surrender everything in order to receive all. Scripture tells us that the kingdom of heaven is taken by force and also that it is within us. When the Lord wants to take possession of his kingdom within us, he must use force if we resist. If we persist in trying to resist or even escape, he withdraws, for, by our fears and refusal to cooperate, we have chosen to endure our purgatory not now, but after death.

(6) We see ourselves, in contrast to the pure blaze of the fire, as "full of evil" and this causes "bitterness" (*Dark Night* 2:10:8) in us, for it is indeed bitter, after all our efforts, to see only darkness and sin, where we had hoped to find Christ enthroned in light and love. We are like the log of wood that is now immersed in "consuming fire" so that no air reaches it. We stifle in our bitter helplessness, unable to believe our purgation is nearly accomplished.

Yet here, too, God usually grants periods of relief when, our vision sharpened by what we have been through and under the influence of Wisdom's discernment, we see that darkness and sin in us are not the final reality. Light and holiness are, and the Spirit has already won over large sections of our foundational self and infused his purity into them.

(7) Near the end of the purifications, joy may be so "ample" that we imagine our sufferings have ended, and we have attained the goal of transformation in love. At the same time a niggling warning tells us that more is in store for us, "a new assault

seems to be threatening" because, out of the corner of our eye, as it were, we glimpse the "root of imperfection which remains" (*Dark Night* 2:10:9).

No one can enter God's presence without being totally clothed in the wedding garment of grace given by him out of his infinite mercy. We have to "put on Christ," or, rather, in terms of the passive purgations, we have to permit Christ to put himself into us. The old man must be replaced by the new man that grace has fashioned.

We must have received the "stone with a new name written on it, known only to the man who receives it" (Rev. 2:17); to have "washed [our] robes white again in the blood of the Lamb" (7:14); to have the Lamb's "name and his Father's name written on [our] foreheads" (14:1).

All this means that we must be not only chosen by God but we must deliberately choose him ourselves. We must be not only clothed outwardly in a wedding garment but have it so drenched in the sacrificial blood of Christ, with which we have mingled our own, that our inner beings have the white purity of perfect love. We must not only be openly named and called by the Father as his but have willingly given up our secret selves to his love's invasion to the point of ravishment.

"It is the most inward part that remains longest unkindled" (*Dark Night* 2:10:9) both in our own depths and in the log's center. With the light given us by the Spirit, we can now clearly see the difference between this area of darkness and the light—and grace-filled spaces around it. It remains there obstinately, a bit like a pile of dirt swept under the carpet that we hope no one will notice. However, under the Spirit's vigilant guidance, we ourselves cannot avoid noticing it, and, as soon as we do, we are consumed with longing to have it cleaned up, so that the Trinity can take total possession.

Grace progresses inward, as in Teresa's mansions. The most interior sufferings are the most excruciating, yet having reached the stage of being almost there, we could not, and have no wish to, turn back. Our one ruling desire is to be completely penetrated by this divine fire, at whatever cost to ourselves, and be with Christ forever.

Having brought us to the brink of full transforming union in this one chapter, John keeps the account of final purification and fulfillment for the following ones. Any readers who have persevered this far in this treatise, and who have understood what is implied because this work is already being carried out in their own souls, will be compelled to read on.

They know for certain that they "do not belong to the night or to darkness" and that "God has called [them] and he will not fail [them]" (1 Thess. 5:5, 24).

Light

Before
there was war
and rumors of war:
now
this immense stillness.

Then
foul smog and swathes
of clammy mists that clung and drenched
the pallor of no-sun,
half light revealing and concealing,
so my eyes' agitated search
that longed to see
vistas of sunlight and clear color
encountered only half-truths
of deceptive gloom.

Now in this holy quiet (dawns
of dereliction and wars' devastation
transmuted) each form, precise and clear,
glows with an aura,
radiance quivering
like new creation's dance
at those primeval words:
"Let there be light!"

Horizons quiver
in coruscations of delight.
The sky's vast dome is filled
with shimmering bliss.

Creation leaps and whirls,
its dance an ecstasy—
and yet
the stillness never stirs,
while deep within
the heart's vast hinterland,
its bomb-cratered wilderness
this glory's gentle consummation
permeates and blesses all.

When the Understanding Is Reduced to Lunacy

Mount Carmel (Summer 1988)

Part I

The mysterious inner self, which we hear about hidden in our physical bodies that can so easily be affirmed through our senses as actual and functioning, cannot be authenticated in the same way. Though within us, it is incorporeal, constantly changing, deceptive, contradictory, revealing extraordinary wisdom and insight at times, and at others a stupidity bordering on idiocy.

All of its aspects interact. It is difficult and mostly impossible to disentangle them. What is real? What is unreal? What arises merely from our emotions? From psychological impulses? From urges and needs buried in the subconscious? Directly from the indwelling Spirit itself? What do we have control over? What are we only unhappy victims of? What is the will anyway? Where is it? How can we be sure something is imagination and not fact? Or vice versa? How open are we to delusion with regard to this universe of inner experience that is so hard to define, locate, and fasten down?

Imagination and fantasy create the craziest improbabilities. Memory persists in either playing tricks or bad jokes or going off on a holiday. The emotions gallop round with the bit in their teeth, irrespective of our hands tugging at the reins. Our irrational and persistent psychological aberrations, quirks, and dislocations insist on being expressed in ways that are both humiliating and at times bizarre. Our intellects abdicate or else connive in thinking up absurdities to encourage them. There is a war inside us, and like St. Paul, we are too often driven to face the fact that we are likely to do the things we hate to do and know we ought not to do, and to leave undone those good things we really want to do. Where is integration, wholeness, peace? Where in all this unfathomable and mysterious inner world does the divine Indwelling dwell?

Hidden somewhere among those manifestations listed above, part of our inner being, influenced by it, working upon it, is the "soul"—and here the Indwelling is. Though this, of course, is itself a metaphor, an actuality beyond human understanding.

All I have been describing by analogy is "the house of the soul." At times it is possessed by exquisite, blissful peace, and repose. At others, all its rooms are in a state of turmoil and disorder, hideous noise and pointless activity. There seems no spot at all where we can sit down quietly and attend to the Lord. We cannot feel he is there anywhere. He seems to have been driven away by a plot that has got out of control.

In reality, this is not so. Deep in the center of this inner house— or maybe in a turret on its roof or maybe way underneath in some cool, remote, totally protected, nuclear-bomb-proof cavern—he remains: inviolable, eternally at rest, and everlastingly active. The ultimate Controller of all the lights gone mad on the switchboard. The Beloved, who cannot, will not be unfaithful.

The graced soul affirms its faith in his Presence, no matter if all awareness or feeling of its actuality is blotted out by the turmoil and revolt in other rooms of the house. We do not feel any comfort at all when we make such faith affirmations. On the contrary, we seem to be spinning madly about like a stray leaf in a whirlwind, and the cacophony deafens us to any still, small voice. And yet…we know and affirm in blind faith and trust that God remains, no matter what.

The above is an attempt to describe, to some extent at least, what we feel like when attacked by a certain kind of inner distress, turmoil, and temptation. Fundamentally, the temptation is against faith and trust. It is a confrontation in aridity with utter absurdity. Just what is the source of the distress and turmoil is hard to pin down, but often it undeniably has a flavor of the diabolic.

We sense this because of several characteristics to do with the long-established nature of our spiritual life and the contrasting nature of what seems to be expressing itself within us at this particular time. These characteristics are as follows:

(1) We have not committed any fully deliberate sin, great or small, for a long time—probably years. On the contrary, we have constantly done all we could to love and serve God and neighbor and to do and suffer his will both actively and passively and in all matters. We have come very close to him in prayer over the years, and our faith has been tried and purified. Yet now we are experiencing God as in fierce opposition to us, a God of wrath and punishment, a destroyer, a maker of war, not peace.

(2) Ordinarily, we lead unspectacular lives, do not seek notoriety, and have sound and rational minds. We have that much-valued asset "common sense," and we tend to be skeptical rather than gullible. At the same time we know and accept that God moves in mysterious and at times extraordinary and startling ways, but we are not expecting him to move like that in us.

Yet now we feel as if we have been set upon by God as a target for the kind of perverse playfulness that a cat exhibits toward a mouse it has captured. God seems to have satanic attributes. Yet how can this possibly be true? It is too absurd. Within us rationality and common sense appear to have abdicated. They have been replaced by what Teresa calls "a raving lunatic" who cannot tell reality from imagination out of control.

(3) We may or may not have a wise, discerning, knowledgeable, and reassuring spiritual guide. If we have not, we have learnt

to rely on and pray constantly for the Spirit's direct guidance, for we are sure God will never forsake his faithful ones. We know from past experience that we have been given the grace to stand fast during severe trials, and we accept the poverty of not having a human guide and comforter, since this is God's will for us at this time. We know what trials and temptations are like. God has helped us weather them before and will continue to do so.

Yet this "whatever it is" has a flavor unlike any other state we have endured. We long and long for a spiritual guide. The irony is that if we should happen to have one already, he is quite likely to say exactly the thing that will disturb us even more deeply. All conviction that our faith is inviolable deserts us. God himself seems to be deliberately stripping us of it. He seems to have abandoned us in our greatest need, and the desolation is awful.

Part II

We do not realize it, but the time has come for the comparatively stable, ordered spiritual state that we have probably been blessed with for some years to be thrown into disarray and even chaos. The purpose is all part of God's plan for our growth in union with him. It is to cause us to die on one spiritual level in order to be reborn on another, higher one. For a long time we shall be quite unable to understand this. In what now happens, there are reminders of God's and Satan's conversations and actions over Job and the aftermath. I take the liberty of paraphrasing the Scripture story somewhat.

> *God*: "Where have you been, Satan?"

> *Satan*: "Oh, round the earth here and there. Roaming about." (There is a peculiar, niggling sense of menace, of mischief likely to happen at any time, leading to catastrophe, in that word "roaming.")

> *God*: "You're bound to have been up to mischief everywhere you've been."

Satan: "I do my best."

God: "You think you're clever and that you can do irreparable damage to my people and my work. But I'm telling you that you won't have any success with my faithful servant, Job. He doesn't fool around with the likes of you. He never puts a foot wrong."

Satan: (jeering) "That's only because you've been on his side all along. You've done so much for him, he's become smug. And he hasn't got the cheek to do anything but cooperate. You just change your tactics and start pitching into him, and he'll soon change his tune. Let me destroy everything you've given him, and he'll start rebelling and cursing you right away. There'll be no "faithful servant" act any longer."

God: "I'll call your bluff. You have my permission to do what you like with his possessions, but don't you dare touch his person."

So Satan "roams" with a purpose and brings a vast catastrophe upon Job that annihilates all his extensive possessions and kills all his family. But Job does not rebel and curse. Instead, he humbly affirms, "The Lord has given and the Lord has taken away. Blessed be the name of the Lord."

Satan returns to God, gloating over what he has accomplished toward Job's downfall, but God is not impressed. As before, he himself taunts Satan by pointing out that though Job has been made destitute, he has not sinned, but on the contrary, retains all his former virtue and remains blameless.

This reminder is a considerable annoyance to Satan, who, being filled with pride and the conviction that he is God's equal, doesn't like to be reminded he is not.

>*Satan*: (sneering) "Virtue! It's only skin deep. No
>doubt he believes you're ready to run and restore
>everything to him. You just see how he'll react if
>I get to work on his body. He'll curse you then.
>I'm daring you to let me."

>*God*: "Permission granted and dare accepted. Af-
>flict his body however your evil imagination sug-
>gests, but you are not—I repeat, not—to kill him."

So Satan covers Job's body with boils, and anyone who has suffered even one good-sized boil will have some faint idea of Job's
misery. He goes and sits in total dejection on the rubbish heap and
isn't helped by his wife's taunts.

>*Wife*: "What's the use of all your virtue, now? Go
>on, curse God and die!"

>*Job*: "Silence, woman! I accepted good fortune
>from God and blessed him for it. Are you telling
>me to stop blessing him just because he sends me
>ill fortune? He's always been the author of his own
>calamities, and he stays in control. And I stay trust-
>ing him."

However, Job has not only a shrewish wife to contend with but
three philosophizing friends who, though they sympathize with him,
are not on the same wavelength at all. In fact, the more they "comfort" him, the more they afflict him. He becomes very depressed
and curses the day he was born.

Satan curses, too, because he has to admit that Job's words
are not the equivalent of cursing God in the way he himself
did. And he's set his heart on reducing Job to his own abysmal level
of wickedness.

Then follows Job's anguished outcry from his bewilderment and
woe, his affirmations and questionings, his spirited responses when
his "comforters" tell him he must be a sinner or God would not do

this to him. He proclaims his innocence. He tells how he experiences God as an implacable, warring enemy. He feels as if God, as well as his so-called friends, is mocking him.

Yet out of this crushing darkness, he persists in reaffirming his faith in God's goodness and his own eventual vindication. At last, from "the heart of the tempest," God speaks to him, puts everything in perspective, and gives him insight into the mysteries of his ways in dealing with his creation. Job repents of all his questioning and inability to understand, and God restores him to an even greater state of blessedness than before.

Part III

There is a parallel between Job and Teresa. In chapter 30 of *The Book of her Life,* she reports on and examines in detail a state of acute inner fragmentation, turmoil, and darkness. This reaches such an intensity that she feels as if she is going mad. There is a kind of crazy agitation within her that has power to unbalance both her mental powers and her emotions.

Much of it she attributes to "the devil," and certainly such disintegration of one's inner being has about it the diabolic flavor of the prince of darkness and lies. One feels intuitively that "an enemy has done it," a spiteful being ruled by absolute malevolence, whose one aim is to destroy our faith and sharing in the indwelling Presence.

At the time of writing about the devil's attacks, Teresa had already experienced countless and varying graces of union with God—for example, the transverberation of her heart in 1559. God had implanted himself deep within her where the enemy could not penetrate, and yet he permitted her to suffer the severest temptations against faith, hope, and trust. Like Job, she had been faithful, virtuous, committed, and blameless. His material riches and possessions of the first phase are paralleled by the spiritual graces God had already given her in great variety and richness before she entered this time of trial.

Neither Job nor she actually died, but both were afflicted with bodily illnesses and the most intense interior trials racking mind, emotions, and spirit in what seemed a frenzy of absurdity. Neither could understand what was happening to them at the time, but later on, when emerged from it, they saw God's action and plan all through it. Job had even more riches restored to him than before. Teresa advanced notably in holiness and received even greater and more exalted graces in prayer.

The severest trials, those that made her feel she was going mad because of their intensity and the inner turmoil and confusion they caused, were preceded by ones not quite as distressing that were caused by bad direction. She had reported to her advisors the visions of Christ she was having, hoping for reassurance, as she always feared delusion. Unfortunately, though holy, prayerful, and well-intentioned, they warned her of diabolic activity and instructed her to repel the visions by a show of contempt and a certain very vulgar gesture. Since she believed she was indeed seeing Christ, to do this caused her the utmost misery. Yet she obeyed them. She felt she was insulting Jesus, even though he himself reassured her (*Life*, ch. 29).

At the same time her fears of delusion persisted, as did the bad advice of her holy mentors. Immersed in anxieties, conflicts, sufferings, extraordinary graces, and humiliating setbacks, she was near the breaking point. Indeed, the spiritual crisis she experienced had some of the symptoms of a nervous breakdown, yet it was predominantly a spiritual trial and the means of her deeper purification and growth in virtue and union with God.

As the crisis deepened, the temptations to distrust herself, her advisors, and even God had a profoundly disturbing effect upon her, even at times bordering on despair. Her mind seemed to be enveloped in a dark stupidity. She could not think straight, be at peace, or evade a tumult of doubts and suspicions about her own spiritual life. A sense of uselessness, paralysis of the will, general malaise, and inability to control her thoughts and direct them toward God would overcome her.

There remained occasions, usually connected with Communion, when the darkness would lift briefly and she would clearly see how stupid and unreal were the fears, obsessions, and unrest that had been possessing her. Then these would return, blotting out all light, rendering her incapable even of praying or thinking of God.

Yet she still had enough self-insight to say, "It is the understanding and the imagination, I think, that are doing me harm here. My will, I believe, is good." Years before, her will had chosen God's will finally and wholly and had been united and blended with it. This sense of union enabled her even under such spiritual stress to be sure that somewhere, somehow, the Presence remained within her, protecting her. Yet she was able to feel almost no comfort.

Her mind (understanding) was out of control and tortured her with its fanciful terrors, endless activity, and interruptions of her prayer and recollection. She regarded it as "a raving lunatic" and records that she had not "sufficient control to keep it quiet for a moment."

Interestingly, in the light of some modern therapeutic techniques, she was able sometimes to disengage and practice nonattachment. She "kept an eye on" this "lunatic," leaving it alone "to see what it would do," even laughing at its antics. At such times she could feel she was no longer its victim, for the Lord himself was "keeping it bound" so that she could once more "enjoy perfect contemplation."

Then back would come the lunatic to possess her, and she would plead with God to set her free from "such bad company" in which she experienced herself as "dispersed in fragments, with each fragment seeming to go its own way." In these few words she encapsulates a psychological state of disintegration well-known to today's psychotherapists. She decides her poor health has something to do with it, and they would probably agree. But she also clearly sees the connection of such fragmentation with the presence of original sin—and here most therapists, not recognizing such a concept, would disagree.

She sees much "false humility" in her attitudes, in her dwelling on her own sinfulness with consequent feelings of guilt. True humility brings "quietness, sweetness, and light," she records, not "turmoil, darkness, aridity," and the experience of God "as of one who is always wielding fire and sword." She is sure it is the devil who produces such effects. (Today's depth psychology may come to a different conclusion.)

She also discerns diabolic activity in her "deep depression," the "stupidity" of her understanding, the torment of her "thousand doubts and suspicions," her fear of being deluded herself and of having deluded her advisors. She is sure that the general disquiet, unrest, turmoil, darkness, affliction, aridity, and sense of being spiritually stifled that oppress her have nothing to do with God's direct action, though he is permitting it to happen.

She sees how the devil has caused her to overreact to trifles that at any other time she would laugh at. He has confused her and made her understanding his own tool to preoccupy her with absurdities and obsessive thoughts. He has clouded her reason, and it is only her well-developed habits of virtue that have enabled her to remain true to God. (Here is an obvious parallel with Job.)

"It has sometimes seemed to me, indeed, that the devils behave though they were playing ball with the soul, so incapable is it of freeing itself from their power. Its sufferings at such a time are indescribable. It goes about in search of relief and God allows it to find none."

She affirms that then the "inward torture…bears some slight resemblance to hell…. What I have learnt is that the Lord is pleased to give him permission and leave to tempt us, just as he gave him leave to tempt Job," she writes.

But, however assiduously the devil works, she knows he cannot kill her faith, though he may well prevent her from deriving any consolation from it. After each trial is over, she sees how he has been active in it, but that now she has been temporarily freed by the Lord from his machinations. For her, one of the worst aspects of the trial is her inability to make any sense of it at the time, or to reassure herself that it will indeed end, or to find reassurance in any other person.

In the attempt to find this comfort and reassurance, she is consumed by a restless search for relief as she strives to recall past graces, convictions, and experiences concerning God. Her addled memory refuses to function, and a frightening lukewarmness takes possession of what was once a most fervent, devoted love of God. A kind of all-pervading stupidity possesses her entire inner self. Spiritual reading is impossible, for the mind refuses to take in anything.

She records that if she attempts conversation, she feels irritable and perverse, though God gives her the grace to refrain from harming or offending others through letting her petulance have free rein.

The general picture is of a thoroughly disorientated person who can do very little to help herself and is forced to be a passive victim till God himself decides enough is enough. It is important to remember that all this happened within a woman obviously chosen and graced by God in a very special way, one who had responded to him ardently and in profound humility, who had suffered greatly in body, mind, and spirit, and learnt to do so meekly and generously. Often, instead of receiving the understanding and support that in desperation she sought from her confessors and advisors, she was belittled, humiliated, told she was deluded, and misunderstood in all important matters.

In the end, relief and rescue came in the person of a saintly Franciscan. God sent her "the blessed Fray Peter of Alcantara." She records,

> I saw, out of his own experience he understood me....
> I needed someone who had gone through it all himself,
> for such a person alone could understand me and inter-
> pret my experiences. He enlightened me wonderfully
> about them.... He left me greatly comforted and very
> happy. (*Life*, ch. 30)

In fact, Fray Peter's summing up of the whole situation was "not to let it trouble" her. Any of it!

Dialogue

"You took your time!" he chided her so tenderly.

"There were barriers all along the route
and someone had tampered with the signposts...."

"But surely you knew this way by heart!
In dreams, if not in actuality. I thought
I'd shown you every bit of it,
taken you along it personally
almost to the end! How could you
have lost your way? Even though
some signposts had been vandalized."

"You'll make me cry!"
        His gentle fingers
stroked her cheek. "You couldn't—
even if you tried. No one ever mourns
or weeps once they've arrived and known
the true embrace, the everlasting kiss of peace."

"The barriers," she whispered, "they were real.
I tore my nails and made my hands all bloody
beating at them. And the muddling signs–
I got confused. I thought that I was going mad.
Storms and darkness. Voices jeering at me
glad that I was lost. And fog...I lost
my shoes. My feet were cut and blistered.
I cried out to you to help me—but
you didn't come. I tell you I was lost.
I called—you didn't answer. You—"

His fingers gently closed her lips.
"Hush now, my dear. My dearest love.
It's all past now. A nightmare. That was all.
A fearful one that blinded you
and made you deaf. And so you could not tell
I never left your side at all. Each moment
I was guiding you through night and storm and fog.
My arm supported you when all the signs
made nonsense. Those barriers you beat at
futilely I led you round by level paths
that wandered over flowery fields where larks sang.
I gave you rest there underneath some trees.
But you were blind and deaf and did not know...
And now you've reached your home. No more
nomad journeys. The search is ended. Can't you feel
the haven of my arms? My heart that beats
for you alone? My eyes that speak of love?
The nightmare's over. Sleep and rest.
Tomorrow we will celebrate together."

She rested then. And slept. At last she slept.

Leaping Into the Abyss

Spiritual Life (Spring 1989)

Part I

In the deepest spiritual cleansings as described by John of the Cross and Jean-Pierre de Caussade, it is stressed that the human intellect must learn to subject itself to, and at times abdicate in favor of, the Spirit's wisdom. Purification through grace opens the way for divine wisdom to be infused into the understanding. We receive the intuitive, spiritual "knowing" that is beyond, yet does not falsify or deny, reason. To attain this knowing we have to travel by the way of faith through the cloud of unknowing that John of the Cross tells us is "thick darkness to the understanding."

Crucifixion of the intellect occurs at the point when darkness is at its most impenetrable and excruciating. Here God is calling us to the ultimate renunciation of the "proprietary use" of our faculty of understanding, as Caussade puts it (Caussade, *On Prayer*, 250–252). Paul expresses it this way: "The Spirit reaches the depths of everything, even the depths of God. After all, the depths of a man can only be known by his own spirit, not by any other man, and in the same way the depths of God can only be known by the Spirit of God" (1 Cor. 2:10–11).

The human intellect, being vulnerable to pride and arrogance, too often believes it knows better than God. Dazzled, we let it convince us that it alone is a sufficient guide to deciding where God is calling us, how he wants us to get there, and when he intends us to arrive at each stage of our journey. But Jesus himself nowhere said, "Blessed are the clever and the know-it-alls, for they will be holy and pleasing to the Father." Instead, he praised faith, love, obedience, humility, simplicity, childlikeness, and devotion to the Father's will.

Thomas Merton provides us with a useful analogy. In Bangkok, not long before his death, he conversed with a Buddhist abbot. Merton asked him, "What is the 'knowledge of freedom'?" The abbot replied, "When you are in Bangkok, you know that you're there. Before that you only knew about Bangkok. One must ascend all the steps, but then when there are no more steps one must make the leap. Knowledge of freedom is the knowledge, the experience, of this leap." (Furlong, *Merton: A Biography*, 322, 324.)

Our intellectual knowledge of God is like "only knowing about Bangkok" and "ascending the steps." The leap into pure faith, the immersion in its dark nothingness, is "knowing that you're there" yet not knowing what or where this is or having any adequate words for it.

The steps can be interpreted as all the past understandings and concepts we have had about God and our union with him. They have been useful aids along our way but are now superfluous and inadequate because they are based only on a partial, flawed vision and fulfillment on a comparatively shallow level. All have to be submitted to the passive purifications of the further reaches of the dark night, and to be let go into the stream of the Spirit's hidden, sanctifying force within. This letting go is the equivalent of the leap into freedom and faith at the top of the steps. It produces a spiritual state of free-floating in space but has to be practiced over and over before the ultimate, irrevocable leap occurs so that liberation becomes permanent. For a long time we make sure we have hold of some rope or other so we cannot leap too far.

On the same trip, Merton commented that we did not so much need liberation from the body as from the mind, i.e., the intellect, in which we are "entangled." Any kind of fixed ideas about God and the spiritual life, especially our own, are likely to be an entanglement, hindering the final leap into the abyss of faith. Many such ideas have evolved because they give spiritual, emotional, or intellectual reassurance. We cling to them involuntarily, and some we cannot relinquish in spite of all our efforts, until we become passive and let God take them from us.

John's fivefold *nada* involves not clinging to anything or anyone at all, except the Divine Being in his unknowable essence and his mysterious but always loving will for us.

The cleverer the intellect and the more fragile the sense of security, the more we are tempted to rationalize until a Celtic knot of interdependent concepts about our personal spiritual life is formed. Its purpose is to protect the psyche from pain and shock. Unfortunately, it also impedes the Spirit's free penetration of that same psyche, so that divine wisdom and purpose cannot implant itself deep down where the springs of action have their source. A palisade of intellectual idols is in the way.

To enter upon this road is to pass on to the goal and to leave one's own way, and to enter upon that which has no way, which is God. For the soul that attains to this state has no longer any ways or methods, still less is it attached to ways and methods, or is capable of being attached to them. I mean ways of understanding, or of perception, or of feeling. Nevertheless it has within itself all ways, after the way of one that possesses nothing yet possesses all things. For, if it have courage to pass beyond its natural limitations, both interiorly and exteriorly, it enters within the limits of the supernatural, which has no way, yet in substance has all ways. (*Ascent* 2:4).

Part II

After struggling for a long time to take the ultimate leap myself, I received a series of enlightenments that I summarized for myself, printed in large letters on a placard and put up in a prominent place in my living space where I would often see it. I found it a most effective practical help, providing I was consistent in applying it to my personal circumstances. Here it is—

SUBMIT TO THE CONFUSION AND MUDDLE OF
not knowing,
not understanding,
not being right.

WAIT FOR THE SPIRIT TO RESOLVE IT

FAST FROM THE "RICHNESS" OF
(emotional security and intellectual sureness)
knowing,
understanding,
being right.

During a period when it seemed that God was reducing my personal life to hopeless absurdity, this program helped me practice abandonment in a constructive and sane way.

In John's "active night," we act by using our wills to consent to confusion, muddle, and the sense of absurdity that arise when the intellect's attempts to reason and understand become submerged in the thick darkness of faith. We learn to submit to all this by a process of "let be, let go, and let God." The trials then persist on one level, while faith takes peaceful charge on another. "For the less the soul works with its own ability, the more securely it journeys, because it journeys more in faith" (*Ascent* 2:1:3).

Faith wants to pervade the rational mind—which knows, understands, seeks to be right—with the seeming irrationality of the divine. God's ways are not our ways, and his justice is other than ours. He is calling us to use our will to oppose the urge and temptation to question and argue with him, asserting our own ideas about what is best to do about all this amorphousness and indefinability.

Genuine security is unexpectedly found in abandonment to darkness, not in feeling safe because we know and understand what is happening. The general rules could well be "don't try to make it happen," "don't hope it will happen again," "don't be afraid it will happen again," "don't attempt to interpret it or lead on from it to 'the next stage,'" "just let it happen and let it stop happening," and "float in it."

Caussade makes a most perceptive and interesting commentary on what he calls "the attachment to the spirit of self-ownership." This blockage to divine action often lurks unrecognized even in those genuinely dedicated to doing and accepting God's will and in those who possess a high degree of spirituality and abandonment. It consists in

> their real independence even, in the usage of the holiest of their powers already consecrated to God in the *matter* of their actions, but not in the *manner* of their performance. Divine love wishes that the actual manner of attributing all to it should depend only on his divine choice, on his pure spirit of grace, with a continual dependence, not only in the interior acts of our own powers but even in the manner of performing those acts; for often God wishes them to be exercised in one fashion and we in another. (Caussade, *On Prayer*, 250–252)

Readiness to make the leap of faith means we are being summoned to an even more radical renunciation of attachment to the manner in which our adherence to his will is practiced. This may entail a change of gear with regard to prayer, vocation, personal relationships, lifestyle, service to others, and experience of God.

Total surrender involves not only submitting in faith to all the ebbs and flows of the Spirit. It also means waiting in patience for God to act, while we fast from our own urges and desires to get moving and to organize matters in a way that seems so obviously right to our understanding.

Such interference on our part results in an intensification of the muddle, confusion, and inability to understand, when the need to feel safe and sure in our thinking is most urgent. This may provide spasms of mental frenzy and thrashing about that, if prolonged, seem to threaten mental breakdown. In contrast, when God is left free to act, the yea-saying action of grace can transport the intellect almost instantaneously from a state of inner turmoil to one of calm lucidity in which supernatural truths are infused, light is everywhere, and a delicate peace encompasses one's whole being. God's action is then momentarily made plain, and peace reigns.

These often violent swings may induce fear of manic-depressive psychosis. At whatever extreme of our inner state, the remedy is a series of acts of abandonment as total as the will can make, based on the "submit-wait-fast" program. We are passive, the Spirit is active. Let her act. Let the intellect be crucified in absurdity. The less we struggle, the less it hurts, and the quicker it will be over. When total inability to understand God's action and purpose is reached, that is the cutoff point, the impasse, the top of the Buddhist steps. We cease trying to fathom what the Spirit is doing or accomplishing, or why, or how. This applies whether the action is taking place in prayer (nonprayer would be a more exact term), personal relationships (crumbling and revealing hollowness), daily life (a series of absurdities, threats, negations, and deprivations), acute interior sufferings (largely the result of our being rigid rather than flexible or limp). As the dentist advises while he drills right on the nerve, "Just relax."

Such diminishments are the means and manner that the Spirit has chosen as the best for leading us to full union. They are all part of the death and rebirth process. They are all graces. They are all adapted to our individual, personal circumstances, just as a garment is made especially to fit one person. We do not have to understand what is happening; we only need to accept and stay still while we let ourselves be moved as when and where God chooses (see *Ascent* 2:16:2).

We need to avoid fiddling with the intellect when what God wants is for it to be left alone so he can deal with it through the passive purgations. To fashion a concept (however holy) in the understanding and then to want with the will what one has created in the mind is to disturb tranquility and block receptivity. Abandonment is present where there is evidence in us of stillness; peace, which is not the same as torpor; enfoldment; love; desirelessness; and sublime, intuitive knowledge given by the Spirit of the purpose of God's confusing action.

Awareness has grown in our minds that concepts, illuminations, messages, holy desires, and the like that come into our thoughts are delivered to a faulty receiving apparatus that, though with love and good will, may misinterpret or misapply them. Also, God may decide to fulfill them in a way other than we, correctly at the time, understood him to mean. This altered course may be because of changed circumstances of which we were unaware, or whose significance we do not realize, or to purify us more efficiently, or to honor God and his will more gloriously, or to answer a developed capacity in us to respond more fully to his love, or to keep our crowning till after we die, making it even more supreme as a result of our patient and purgatorial waiting.

If we submit, wait, and fast, we shall not be dismayed when God's revelations to us personally are altered, withdrawn, or not fulfilled in the way expected. He chooses the way and the time, the how and when, the whether or not. We may speculate (detachedly), but never cling to rigid ideas and convictions about the Spirit's action in us and our lives. She may infuse a deeper understanding when she knows we are capable of grasping it and of opening ourselves to her plan in the matter. The intellect, at this stage of the spiritual life, is called to submit completely to the fact that God alone knows best, whereas we are tangled up in not knowing, not understanding, and not being right.

It is impossible to understand the hidden truths of God that are in his sayings and the multitude of their meanings. He speaks according to the way of eternity. We understand only the ways of flesh and time (*Ascent* 2:20:5). For us the solution is to be so abandoned that we float weightlessly in his will and wisdom as they exist in eternity and infinity, relinquishing the need to understand. This, paradoxically, is freedom (the idea of "floating" in the abyss of faith always seems to me less suicidal than that of "leaping into"). Such weightlessness is the result of nonidentification with personal fears, anxieties, clutchings for emotional and intellectual security, urges to know and understand, disturbances about not being right, humiliations at being wrong and making mistakes and being stupid, suffering and frustration over being denied what we believed God has promised, dismay at absurdity and meaninglessness, and rebellions at the apparent contradictions in the divine action.

The serene floating in the divine will and action that is the result of such a crucifixion of the intellect could well be the true levitation, because it is purely spiritual and interior.

Part III

Some of the specific areas in which the Spirit is likely to be active to remove impediments that prevent such free-floating of the understanding are the following:

Delusions. These are sincerely held and often obstinately so. Some people are gifted with a "natural facility" through which their "many tastes and affections and the operations of their faculties are fixed upon God and spiritual things." Because of this, they think they are receiving "spiritual blessings" directly from God when really they have manufactured them for themselves. They tend to treasure and cling to them as personal possessions (which they are), especially given them by God (though they have not been) (See *Dark Night* 2:16:5).

The Spirit is working to produce a genuine transformation in which all spiritual blessings will originate from her and be infused into us by her action. For this to happen, the gifts and graces we think up for ourselves and, as it were, bestow upon ourselves have to be deprived of their force until "they have no more strength," for "when the soul is making most progress, it is traveling in darkness, knowing naught" (*Dark Night* 2:16:6, 8).

Delusions can be very subtle and deep-seated. They are open to diabolic manipulation. The remedy is self-distrust and scepticism, coupled with trust in God and guileless openness with one's spiritual guide. As delusions are stripped away, the mind is opened up and emptied of its attachments to distortions of the truth. Then Wisdom herself can enter to occupy the place God has prepared for her.

Rationalizations. These fulfill our personal want and need to be sure we are in the right, while they keep our conscience clear. A good name for them is "clever talk." When they are elaborate, they can form an efficient cover over dubious motives and self-indulgences, much as surface camouflage conceals the hideout of a nuclear missile.

Constructing rationalizations can keep the intellect so busy and preoccupied that faith and contemplation are inhibited. The rationalization has a compulsion to be in the right and get its own way. This urge may be rooted in repressed needs and compulsions, yet one of the purposes of the passive purgations is to arouse and exacerbate such insecurities until we have no recourse but to turn them, their destructive effects, and our whole lives over to God.

Unconscious, obsessive drives get in our way and in God's, trying to influence "the manner of our performance," yet because of their strength and concealment are usually beyond our power to locate and eradicate without professional help. If only we take that leap into the abyss as fully as we are able, the Divine Therapist will get us into right order much more effectively and deeply than any human one, no matter how well qualified.

Rationalizations comfort and reassure us that all is well, but God wants us to face the fact that, in spite of our sincere efforts, all is far from well. Besides this, they are a distortion, whether subtle or gross, of the truth of our relationship with God. They try to convince us, "I'm OK. I don't need you tampering with my life, God. I'm not doing anything wrong."

Ideals. It may seem strange to suggest that part of our mental equipment that needs to be cast away at the top of the steps is our genuine ideals and idealizations. Until we let the Spirit take over our intellects, we do not realize that we are trammeled by concepts derived from our human needs and that we have no proof that even the most precious and elevated of them has been implanted in us by the Spirit.

It is true that grace takes over and perfects nature, but there is a grey area here. We have almost certainly warped nature because our understanding is so limited, is so often also warped, and is governed probably by our drive for self-fulfillment in the manner of our own choice.

In the past, ideals may have helped us renounce the base and strive for the exalted. Their usefulness is over once we have entered the midnight of faith. Here they are ballast to be jettisoned. Only God can choose for each of us what is to be our particular highest goal and fulfillment. The process of idealization of other human beings, however good and even holy they may undeniably be, is always a distortion of the truth, for all goodness and holiness come from God, and it is to him that the thanks, praise, and adoration are due. "Why do you call me good? Only God is good," Jesus rebuked.

Ideals can also lead to immoderate commitment to and involvement in "causes" with consequent distortion of judgment and a lapse from devotion to God's will for itself alone. Rationalizations that we are doing his will, that this "cause" will therefore prosper, and the ideal it holds out as its end will be victorious over a variety of self-seekings and evasions of the truth.

In passive purgations of the understanding, the Spirit cleanses us from our ideals and idealizations through disillusionment, defeats, broken relationships, lost causes, betrayals, and bleak self-insights.

Fantasies. The imagination and memory cling to the past, adorn the present, and construct scenarios for the future. All of these are distortions of the truth and encrustations on the intellect marring the simplicity of pure faith.

Fantasies also arise from our own buried needs, lacks, compulsions, and obsessions. We cannot let go because we need to be reassured. Seeking reassurance, we reconstruct the past so that it is more emotionally satisfying, puts us more obviously in the right, humiliates those who have belittled us, or shores up our lack of confidence by presenting defeat as disguised success. Some fantasies of the past are played over and over like records stuck in a groove or repeat programs in a twenty-four-hour cinema.

We decorate the present by imposing our own interpretations and wish fulfillments on what is happening. We escape from facing it as it is by evasive action consisting of a series of sidesteps and backward movements away from the bare truth. We imagine to be there what is not present and let memories of the past interpose themselves between us and the actuality of the present moment.

Jesus stressed the importance of living in the present moment. Caussade points out that the present moment is, or ought to be, a sacrament, because it is the only moment in time in which divine providence is wholly present to us. By the wrong use of fantasy, we befoul this sacrament and shut ourselves off from its blessings.

We cannot know the future, yet we persistently fantasize about it. We hook up memories of the past and decide the future will be an embellishment of these. If the memories are unpleasant and painful, we dread the future. If happy and fulfilling, we disregard the reality of the present and project ourselves into an imagined scenario that is even more ecstatic.

The degree of danger in all this is in proportion to its willfulness. If we struggle against deliberate consent to and indulgence in it, we show the Spirit we are inviting her to cleanse us passively of all such nonsense. A genuine, profound love of and search for the truth, as God sees it, provides a powerful counterbalance to overindulgence in a harmful use of memory and imagination in fantasy (In this I am not, of course, questioning the creative use of fantasy, memory, and imagination in the arts, where its results can be gloriously positive).

Patterns and Maps. We make these for ourselves in both useful and harmful ways. A detached clinical examination of our life experience and our spiritual development, if prayerfully, humbly, and unobsessively done, will usually reveal repetitive patterns. These indicate areas of weakness and strength; places where grace has been at work in, on, and through us maybe for years; compulsive syndromes of behavior harmful to spiritual development; blockages to growth evincing themselves in persistent disasters and setbacks. If such examinations are done not in morbid introspection (which is disguised self-love) but prayerfully in the Spirit, asking for enlightenment, they amount to a meticulous examination of conscience.

The danger comes when we are so unaware of our behavior patterns, their nature and effects, that we let them unconsciously influence us into making life maps. Once the maps are drawn, we feel safe only when we adhere to them. We become rigid and ossified. We grind to a halt spiritually and are closed to the Spirit's entry and her gift of interior renewal.

If under all this God finds a will that truly longs for him but is powerless because of indeliberate hardening of the spiritual arteries (to vary the map metaphor), he may send the kind of grace that registers on us as cataclysmic. There is a mental or emotional collapse, a deviation into bizarre behavior, acute anxiety attacks, outbursts of passionate revolt, or some other unexpected upheaval. Its effect on the psyche is like that of a scale-six earthquake on landforms. It breaks up the established pattern of roads, fences, building, rivers, hills, and valleys, obliterating the familiar. Old routes are no longer operable, so new ones have to be found, followed and established as functional.

This kind of happening—in reality God's own kind of "shock treatment" tailored by him to our individual, special needs—can be part of the passive purgations of the understanding for some people. They are then in great need of spiritual support and the guidance and reassurance of an expert director who is also knowledgeable in depth psychology.

Inner Talking. This is a common aspect of misuse of memory and imagination and an enemy of that inner stillness necessary for contemplation. Dialogues or long speeches of self-justification; endless repetition of slogans, tags of approval or disapproval tied on us by others or on them by us; grief-stricken reproaches and recriminations; declarations of love; pleadings for understanding; angry accusations—these and many variations of them invade the mind like a swarm of insects that wheel and dart at whim incessantly.

Because they are often obsessive and compulsive, such invasions are difficult or impossible to control by will and are commonly called "distractions," which, of course, they are. The origin of their persistence is outside consciousness, though they may relate directly to recent, remembered, and often painful or elating happenings. A person hooked on inner talking usually sits with a fixed, unblinking gaze oblivious of real surroundings, absorbed in the repetitive hidden drama.

Consciousness of what is happening and a deliberate effort to dissociate from it by turning the mind to prayer or constructive, controlled thinking, or by directing the attention outward, or by

making conscious, frequent acts of abandonment, need to be cultivated. If this proves impossible, a dive deep down underneath the
commotion can be attempted, a sinking into faith's thick darkness
where God is below the intellect and all its gyrations and clever
talk. Here inner talking becomes irrelevant, and in ceasing to pay
attention to it, we find that the clamor and voices die away.

This kind of mental activity during the deeper cleansings of the
dark night is a trial and a temptation, often very hard to bear, not a
deliberate fault. It can even be intense and persistent enough to
amount to an affliction.

Through doggedly persisting in the attempt to detach ourselves,
we grow in recollection of the will (which is the deepest kind of
recollection) in spite of lack of it in the mind. If we wait in abandonment for deliverance, the Spirit eventually infuses another kind
of recollection in which stillness invades all the faculties so that
all this nonsensical, unproductive inner talk ceases before awareness of God's holy presence and love.

Projections. These are figurative, fancy dresses that we impose
on other people and even on God and then treat the disguises as if
they were truth. The fancy dresses really belong to us, but we
prefer not to admit to ourselves that they do. We hide them away
in dark, locked closets and repress all awareness of them. These
garments are aspects of ourselves we disapprove of because they
may have been the cause of adults' rejection, condemnation, and
cruelty toward us in our early childhood. We learned then that it
was safer to hide these aspects and act as if they did not exist.
However, they have retained a dangerous potency. We relieve the
inner pressures they engender by clothing other people in our own
fancy dresses, while we criticize and condemn these scapegoats
for their vile tempers, foul tongues, dirty minds, dishonest ways,
meanness, self-centeredness, boasting, pharisaism, and so on. In
this way we castigate others for our own unfaced faults, sins, and
unpleasant tendencies. It has been wisely said that if you want
to know what your own faults are, observe what you are often

condemning in other people. Whenever there is overreaction, fanaticism, blanket condemnation, double standards, and hypocrisy, we can suspect projection and repression.

Jesus had clear insight into this problem when confronted with the woman taken in adultery by her self-righteous captors. Perhaps he knew that secretly, deep in their own hearts, they desired her sexually themselves, so he said, "Let him who is without sin cast the first stone." It is to be assumed they stole away one by one because the Spirit momentarily gave each of them a humiliating glimpse of the fornicator's fancy dress hidden in their own closet. Thus their self-understanding received a true, though unwelcome, enlargement.

Projections are psychological rather than intellectual phenomena, yet they warp our understanding of ourselves and others. It is through the intellect that the Spirit is going to give us knowledge of them in the passive purgations. With these painful self-insights, she will also offer the grace to face and accept them, but we have to muster the humility and courage to do so. If we react positively, we shall have absorbed a little more of divine wisdom and, in the self-knowledge given by it, shall be able to say and mean, "There, but for the grace of God, go I," instead of imposing our own fancy dresses upon others' reality.

Part IV

In all purifying transactions between the Spirit and our spiritually ailing selves, a wise, patient, kind, but implacable confessor is invaluable. Once we can present frankly in the reconciliation room the reprehensible elements we have (probably involuntarily) concealed within ourselves for so long, we are released to open ourselves even more to the divine invasion.

Such a process of self-revelation is crucifying to self-love and should take place stage by stage as we grow strong enough in grace to endure it. To force the procedure is again to try to impose upon

God our own ideas of the how and when and the manner of his dealing with us.

Purification of the understanding entails the exposure and casting out of all lies we are living in regard both to ourselves and to others. The mechanisms detailed above belong among those lies, but since they are usually props to the insecure, they must not be removed until grace has given the inner strength to withstand the shocks entailed.

Whatever impedes the inflowing of God into our depths hinders our growth in faith and contemplation. As long as we are captive to any of the blockages detailed here, we will not be able to be fully subject to holy wisdom but will always be interposing our own ideas and concepts. We shall want to organize and manage both God and our own lives, spiritual and material, instead of letting his will and divine providence fashion them in the way he wants. We will lack that inner stillness that opens up a dwelling place for the Trinity. We will be incapable of the leap into the abyss.

Perhaps a quotation from John of the Cross can best summarize the matter:

> It is so difficult to find the truth. For that which is most clear and true is to us most dark and doubtful; wherefore, though it is the thing that is most needful for us, we flee from it. And that which gives the greatest light and satisfaction to our eyes we embrace and pursue, though it be the worst thing for us, and make us fall at every step. In what peril and fear does man live, since the very natural light of his eyes by which he has to guide himself is the first light that dazzles him and leads him astray on his road to God! And if he is to know with certainty by what road he travels, he must perforce keep his eyes closed and walk in darkness, that he may be secure from the enemies who inhabit his own house. (*Dark Night* 2:16:12)

Caught

You have the power to cast your line
into the Tuscarora deep. It sinks
dark fathoms for long nights on end.
Its barbed hooks become embedded in
cliff faces plunging to the center of the earth.

O fisherman so practiced in your art
does your finger casually extended
feel the twitch of the responsive line?
A message vibrating upward from dank depths
where subterranean earthquakes take their origin?

The monsters stir outraged at this invasion.
The waters swirl at their immense commotion
Your line is tangled in the slimy serpent's wrath
your hook is wrenched about in vast upheaval.

The barb stabs deeper. It cannot be dislodged.

Of Oak Trees and Submarines: Reflections on the Dark Night

Spiritual Life (Spring 1990)

The purpose of the dark night, according to St. John of the Cross, is to lead us into the full day of perfect loving union with the Trinity. This means that we merge with Christ in all his resurrection glory and joy, though in this life these attributes will manifest themselves only intermittently and mutedly, for we are still confined by the limitations of our physical existence. Faith in the reality of this full union, hope that Jesus will lead us into it if only we follow him trustingly all the way to the tomb, and the unconditional love of our as yet imperfect hearts—these are the attributes that through the dark night "join Beloved with lover, lover transformed in the Beloved," as John puts it in his poem, "In one dark night."

During these necessarily passive nights, grace penetrates all levels of our inner being to eliminate every trace of sin. It invades—as long as we stay receptive—those deeply rooted, perverted tendencies for which we are not personally responsible, but which do influence our behavior and attitudes in numerous unloving and even evil ways (At this stage of the spiritual journey there is no *deliberate* evil action, but indeliberate blindness to others' serious needs can well operate because of some hidden complex of insecurity, anxiety, or the like).

Pulling Up Roots

In the so-called "active nights," we purposefully do what we can, with the help of grace, to accomplish the cleansing, and in fact we must persevere in such activity till death. In the passive nights, divine help and activity penetrate where we cannot to reach those stubbornly embedded roots of sin so that they are either wrenched out or dissolved away.

To use a gardening analogy—we can easily deal with bedding plants, whether flowers or vegetables, using handforks and trowels or larger forks and spades. If we labor hard enough, we can even dig up some of the bigger shrubs and small trees with perhaps a heavier shovel and fork and a grubbing tool.

But what do we do about an oak or pine tree? True, it can be cut down and the stump burned out, using more advanced power tools and a number of skilled helpers. But say for some good reason we want to have the whole tree taken out by the roots. In that case, outside help and implements like tractors, mechanical diggers, and maybe explosives, together with experts to use them, have to be employed. We can only stand back and let it happen, though it is true we ourselves have initiated the procedure. For whatever reason, we want it done.

Similarly, in the deeper passive nights, we have to invite God in to do the work for us, because our own tools and strength are inadequate. This invitation may itself be more passive than active, in that we may not clearly realize in the intellect what our heart is saying to God, but its motive is always love and only love.

This means we do not want to be cleansed just so we can self-righteously admire our own virtues and, satisfied with what we see, set about planning our exact place in heaven (near the throne, of course), much as we would choose a prime site for our palatial new home with all modern conveniences. Nor does it mean our chief motive is an urgent desire to escape the pains of hell.

Rather, the love motive wants the ultimate cleansing for quite different ends. It longs to be used by God to give him honor and glory and to share in Christ's redemptive work for others, to become a perfectly adaptable tool for Jesus to use in his ongoing work in the world. It wants to be a channel cleared of all debris and pollution so that, through it, divine love can pour living waters into the world for healing of humanity's wounds. It longs for every obstruction to this in-and-out flowing to be removed, if need be by divine force and through its own agony.

It wants to be made a kind of compelling advertisement for the power of divine grace over human weakness. In its humility and self-awareness of its own inadequacy and unworthiness, it wants others to see it as it is and exclaim, "If God can do that for her—and we all know what she's like—then there is hope for me!" It wants these others to catch its own insatiable thirst for grace and so become reckless in their longing for God and their readiness to suffer all and even die in order to be purged and so reach full love-union with him.

A Pure Heart Create in Me, O God (Ps. 51:12)

The purified heart that has been finally and fully claimed by God can, paradoxically, become progressively purer and more fulfilled in him right till the moment of death. This is because God himself expands its capacity with his inpouring love, fills the enlarged space with more love, which expands it further—and so the process goes on. But never without our full consent. A helpful prayer is "My God, penetrate and possess me to the uttermost—and don't take any notice when I squeal in pain."

It is fear of suffering that holds back so many from the unqualified gift of themselves to God, so that he can do whatever he likes with them. But has he not promised he will match every trial with enough grace to bear it? Of course this may well mean that part of the trial will be the experience of desperately needing more, and more, and more grace.

However, this in itself provokes a constant plea for what we know we cannot endure without. It engenders intimate knowledge of our own helplessness—"Without Christ I can do nothing" (cf. John 15:5)—coupled with a reckless confidence—"With God all things are possible" (Mark 10:27). "I can do all things in Christ who strengthens me."

The truth is that grace can be flooding into us while we remain unaware of it and experience no comfort. This happens because we are only too prone to think, as soon as we realize we are overcoming, "Aha! I'm getting somewhere! I've conquered! How brave and strong I am! How far I've advanced in virtue! I hope everyone else is noticing all this!"

Such self-congratulations and the tendency to various forms of self-exaltation arise from those buried roots that only the passive purgations can eradicate. So God's work progresses in direct relation to our own humble receptivity to grace, and humility, as is well known by the humble, comes above all through dire humiliations. What appears to be the curse of being refused the grace we need is really the blessing of being given it in abundance, but minus the extra grace of the awareness to enjoy it. Being what we are, this last grace would engender pride. Only those with great humility dare say, "He who is mighty has done great things to me" (Luke 1:49).

Waiting in Hope

It is excruciatingly humiliating to self-love and self-will to have to admit, "I can't go on unless I get help. I can't bear anymore without some special grace. I'm beaten to the ground and I haven't a hope of even getting to my knees unless you yourself raise me up, my God." Our refuge is Christ in his passion, crucifixion, death, and entombment—above all in his cry of dereliction on the cross.

In such depth-charge trials, the negative emotions take over, and the will to endure seems swamped by them. "All your waves and billows have gone over me" (Ps. 42:8)…"My God, my God, why have you forsaken me?" (Ps. 22:2).

We have to work out a technique for somehow disregarding the emotional turmoil long enough to tune into the will. The will is like a submarine, resting on the seabed far beneath all the surface commotion of the hurricane, while it keeps on throbbing mesmerically, "I believe. I hope. I trust. My God, I rest in your everlasting arms of love and know for certain I am safe."

At the end Jesus cried out, "Into your hands I commend my spirit" (Luke 23:46)—we can add, "and all my affairs, and my whole life, and this awful sense of being violently expunged out of existence!"

The point is that once we have reached this depth of the passive purgations, the will has long since been made captive in God's will. We are where we are precisely because we have given him carte blanche to do what he likes with us. In response he has said, "All right. I'll use your precious gift of yourself and your deepest will as the means of bringing you into the supreme, loveing union of all with me. Just let me act while you stay passive, and all will be well. All is well."

It is this last affirmation, "All is well," that the dogged, consecrated will monotonously keeps on affirming from its grounding on the seabed. "No matter what you do with me…. Even though you come to me as an avenging warrior…an annihilating tempest…an implacable enemy…a nuclear bomb…yet will I believe. I believe. I trust. I hope. If you destroy this temple it is only so you can raise up a glorious everlasting one in three days on the same site. I give you my authority to go on with your work in whatever way you see fit. You know best and you never make mistakes. I'll wait in the darkness and stuffiness. You will come in the end. In fact, you're with me all the time, and your loving arms never cease to hold me against your heart. Your love is everlasting, and I am safe for ever in it."

To sum up:

> The soul cannot come to this union without great purity, and this purity is not gained without great detachment from every created thing and sharp mortification. This is signified by the stripping of the Bride of her mantle and by her being wounded by night as she sought and went after her Spouse; for the new mantle which belonged to the betrothal could not be put on until the old mantle was stripped off. Wherefore, he that refuses to go forth in the night aforementioned to seek the Beloved, and to be stripped of his own will and to be mortified, but seeks him upon his bed and at his own convenience, as did the Bride, will not succeed in finding him. For this soul says of itself that it found him by going forth in the dark and with yearnings of love. (*Dark Night* 2:24:4)

Candle and Pinecone Sequence

This flame's shape is like a spear—
or else a dagger—leaving wounds concealed
behind the bulwark of the living flames of love,
which do not burn.

Lights illuminate our darknesses
and flames give warmth—though the uncircumspect
receive what could be stigmata, exposed
or else concealed in heart, or brain, or bloodless hands.

This flame's symmetry is like a spear's keen blade
or else a dagger, small but dangerous,
shaped to deal out penetrating wounds
mysteriously secret, all of them
deep buried in the heart's blind fastnesses
spousal gifts from those living flames of love.

The Emptiness Within

Review for Religious (September/October 1990)

Ours is an age of space-consciousness and space exploration. These have induced an awareness of a limitless beyond that can be terrifying. We know that in space, universe extends beyond universe in an infinitude of expanding galaxies. The immensity is beyond our comprehension.

Ours is also an age of inner exploration of our own human psyche. Depth psychology probes level on level of inner awareness, submerged awareness, and nonawareness. These probings link up with that aspect of spirituality that mystically intuits the indwelling of the Trinity, the homeliness of God in us that Jesus spoke of and promised to his faithful followers the night before he died.

Just as there is endless mystery in the outer universe, so there is in the inner one. God dwells in us—if we long for him and prepare our spiritual house to receive him. Not only that, but he permeates our inner being further and further as we open ourselves to receive him.

"How rich are the depths of God!" exclaimed St. Paul. And it is these very depths that merge with our own through the divine penetration and the graces it brings.

This is by no means always a consoling experience. On the contrary, it can seem to hurl us into an abyss of unmeaning that is caused by our incapacity to understand divine meaning and purpose in all their infinite inclusiveness. Only faith can cope with the apparent absurdity, and too often in this state we experience ourselves as lamentably lacking in faith.

In this article I examine and comment on this negative aspect of divine and human intermingling by using the concept of "the inner void."

Normally, we human beings fill our days and nights with the business of living, working, playing, and social interchange. This is the way it has to be if society is to continue and be dynamic. For committed Christians this day-to-day living and doing is permeated with another dimension—that of being-in-Christ. The more fully they relate mundane activities to loving and serving the Lord, the more Christocentric their lives become. The more they cleave to him, the more the Trinity enters into their inner selves through the purity of their intentions, so that they truly become temples of the Holy Spirit. A pure intention is one that is centered on what Jesus stressed must be our fundamental option—"God's will, not mine, because I love him with my whole being." Strangely, the intensity of such a single-minded love can lead not to a blissful sense of fulfillment, but to its opposite—an experience of crucifying inner emptiness, a void of unappeasable longing crying out for a God who appears not to care or even answer. How much longer will you forget me, Yahweh? Forever? How much longer will you hide your face from me? How much longer must I endure grief in my soul and sorrow in my heart by day and by night? (Ps. 13:1–2).

The ache for God, disguised as it may be in a multitude of ways, seems to be endemic to the human heart. In Christ's followers it can become so insistent that it rules their lives. After many years of loving, faithful service to this object of their desire, a paradoxical inner state is likely to develop. The searcher for the pearl of great price and of the glorious liberty of the sons and daughters of God, though consumed with an intolerable yearning for God, now experiences him as absent just when he is loved and longed for most. This is usually a sign of the call to a much deeper relationship with him, one that has a different quality from any that preceded it.

We are drawn by the Spirit into this state of being when all created things have lost their power to compel or fulfill us. We have learned, often in bitterness and pain, that none of them can supply anything but a temporary and partial satisfaction. Behind and through them we have kept glimpsing their Creator, and now he fills our vision and summons us to come closer.

We have begun floating in our inner void, sure at last that only his love can fill it. Aware that he is calling and drawing us, we want with all our will to respond, yet we remain thwarted. Yearn and strive as we may, we can neither reach nor receive him. Empty and grieving, we experience him as the absentee God, yet we have never in our lives been more free of sin and fuller of love than we now are. Why has this void opened at the very time when we are possessed by love-longing for God? To anyone familiar with the inner depth reality of the subconscious and unconscious, the answer will make sense.

The roots of our attachments to what God has created and the causes of our persistence in letting them come between us and him are still buried deep within us. They fasten us down to where we are so that we are unable to soar in freedom to him. Though we have done all in our power, with the help of grace, to love and serve him and though deliberate sin of any kind has long been eliminated from our living, the roots of sinful tendencies remain there hidden away, so that we are not even conscious of them. We cannot locate or name them, let alone wrench them out or dissolve them away. In our impotence and humiliation, we gradually realize only God can do this through his own mighty love and the grace he pours into us through his Spirit.

Only his action can gradually dilate our hearts so that they are able to receive more and more of what he offers. Only his grace can penetrate into our subconscious to reveal what is concealed there. Only it can in various ways impel upward into consciousness what is hidden. Only his Spirit of Wisdom knows, and can reveal to us in ways we can accept, what must be made conscious and purified if we are to enter into full union with the Trinity.

By invading our depths, the Spirit is not violating our free will, for God knows our longing for him is such that at last we are prepared to let him have his way with us, no matter how much it hurts. "Oh God, my God, for you my heart yearns, like a dry, weary land without water" (Ps. 63:1).

God's answer to our yearnings is to fill our void with himself. This process is purgatorial. After death we pass outside time and space into eternity and infinity. If at this transition we are not already filled with God, our void goes with us. No one has returned to tell us how God deals with it then, but traditionally the Church has taught the doctrines of purgatory (a cleansing process through which grace fits us to receive and behold God) and hell, where our void remains just that forever. All those, known and unknown, who have become saints before they died, have had their voids filled with God in this life. Some have left records of what their experience was like, and these indicate something at least of what they endured under the Spirit's ruthless but perfectly loving action.

St. John of the Cross's testimony is probably the most authoritative, instructive, and detailed. After stressing that this state of purification is one of darkness and pure faith, he elaborates as below:

> The Divine assails the soul in order to renew it and thus to make it Divine; and, stripping it of the habitual affections and attachments of the old man, to which it is very closely united, knit together and conformed, destroys and consumes its spiritual substance, and absorbs it in deep and profound darkness. As a result of this, the soul feels itself to be perishing and melting

> away in the presence and sight of its miseries, in a cruel spiritual death, even as if it had been swallowed by a beast (as Jonas was)…[and] in this sepulcher of dark death it must needs abide until the spiritual resurrection which it hopes for.
>
> …But what the sorrowful soul feels most in this condition is its clear perception as it thinks that God has abandoned it, and, in his abhorrence of it, has flung it into darkness. It is a grave and piteous grief for it to believe that God has forsaken it…. For indeed when this purgative contemplation is most severe, the soul feels very keenly the shadow of death and the lamentations of death and the pains of hell, which consist in its feeling itself to be without God, and chastised and cast out, and unworthy of him; and it feels that he is wroth with it. (*Dark Night* 2:6:1, 2)

The intensity and pain of this inner experience of the void will vary according to the strength and depths of our sin-roots, the greatness of our love and longing for God, our perseverance and abandonment during the process, and the degree of holiness (or wedding-garment splendor and soaring freedom) that God intends for each sufferer. This purpose of his is, of course, hidden in the mystery of his endless love, of which the void itself is but one aspect.

If the void is endured until the process of cleansing and freeing is completed, we have been through and emerged from our own personal purgatory. We are united with the Trinity in what has been called "transforming union" ("I live, now not I, but Christ lives in me") or "the spiritual marriage."

"Alleluia! The reign of the Lord our God the Almighty has begun. Let us be glad and joyful and give praise to God, because this is the time for the marriage of the Lamb. His bride is ready, and she has been able to dress herself in dazzling white linen, because her linen is made of the good deeds of the saints" (Rev. 19:7–8).

Our void has been emptied of self and filled with Christ. What are some of the hallmarks of this emptying and filling of the void, in the here and now? Here is a commentary on a few of the main ones.

1. *Helpless Waiting.* In the void we have no alternative but to wait. I think of Mary between the annunciation and the birth of Jesus. She knew she had conceived and that the Christ of God was growing and developing within her, but the process was and had to remain hidden and secret.

What she did not know was exactly what and who the child would prove to be. God was at work in her, and she was cooperating passively, through her *fiat*, by letting it happen and trusting him about the outcome of his labors. She was "full of grace," and so the whole process was under the Spirit's complete control. Her personal contribution was to stay still and see what eventuated.

⁂ Once the void opens in us, we too must wait while Christ is formed in us in his fullness. We continue to live and love as Christians, to serve God and neighbor in our work, personal relationships, duties, and offerings, all aimed at renewing the temporal order and purifying our lives from self-love and self-seeking. We have been doing these things for a long time and had assumed we would be persevering in them in much the same way until death. We do persevere, but not "in the same way."

⁂ For now the void is there, and we begin to enter a new dimension and level of being. Gradually grace enlightens us so that we understand something of what still needs to be done in our inner depths to open us to God so he can penetrate further. At the same time we are shown how it is beyond our own capacity and resources to bring about such a self-exposure.

A chasm of helplessness and poverty gapes within us. We realize that in our frozen immobility, we are still able to act in one specific way. We can let God act and stay passive ourselves. We can let him do the unveiling and the choosing for us and in us in his own way and time. Our role is to surrender and wait and wait and wait.

Waiting is a difficult art to learn and practice in our frenetically active and materialistic age. Neither our environment, education nor life aims and circumstances have prepared us for it. Though we try, we go on failing, because we cannot help interfering with God in spite of our best intentions. Humbled, we learn that only grace can enable us to learn this painful art. Under its influence, we slowly begin to relax and be still, and our void gently opens wider in faith, trust, and hope. We realize how important patience is, how lost we are if God does not help us, how he does not and cannot do so unless we deliberately exercise our free will and let him. Here the active and the passive merge.

As we go on waiting, our helplessness deepens into a sense of impotence. We are rather like quadriplegics who must depend on others for most of their needs. If they are not to be consumed with self-pity and rage, they must turn the necessary waiting that forms an indelible part of their lives into an art.

We ourselves are not waiting for other people to help us, but for God. "I waited and waited for Yahweh. Now at last he has stooped to me and heard my cry for help" (Ps. 40:1).

2. *Longing for God.* Thirst for God consumes us in this state. "As a doe longs for running streams, so longs my soul for you, my God. My soul thirsts for God, the God of my life" (Ps. 42:1–2). We are like "a dry, weary land without water" (Ps. 63:1).

When two lovers are parted, they long ardently and painfully for each other's presence. In the void we experience God as an absentee God, even as one who spurns us. We are hopelessly in love with him—we would not have been invited by the Spirit into this level of being were it not so—yet he seems to be denying himself to us, to be teasing us cruelly on purpose.

We know he is there, believe this is so, and in some indescribably formless way even experience him as indeed with us, enfolding us, and yet we never seem to reach or catch sight of him. In his absence we have faith he is present, but this is no comfort. It is like being alone in a completely dark room, yet having an intuitive awareness of another Presence with us in the same enclosed space. We cannot see or touch him or even hear his breathing. Yet, shiveringly, we are completely certain Someone is with us.

Perhaps because of this strange certainty, our longing that is never appeased intensifies until it possesses us. This absentee yet ever-present God and Lover we experience as capricious, so that our longing is a form of bitter suffering, and often we have to struggle against feelings of resentment and hopelessness. We challenge him, "It is you, God, who are my shelter. Why do you abandon me?" (Ps. 43:2).

There is no answer, no comfort. The silence is absolute, our hunger unappeased. In the end, we become dumb. Our patience in waiting has deepened as our longing intensified. We understand the time for consummation is not yet, for we are not ready. We see that our longing is a grace, given to us so we will more readily submit to an even more radical emptying out. We have not yet reached that total nakedness of unselfish love that will indicate our readiness to be clothed in Christ.

We have yet to long for this for his sake, his honor and glory, the fulfilling of his incarnational aims, instead of for our own self-gratification and our pleasure in our own "holiness." At last we understand that our motives need radical purification, for they are laced together everywhere by tenuous, yet tough, strands of self-love and self-will.

All holiness is God's. Of ourselves we have none until we have put on Christ and can glory in his glory and love with his love. Our longing is being purified till this is what we truly want above all else.

3. *Loss of Meaning and Purpose.* Whether it is a cause or a result of the void is hard to say, but a hallmark of this state is loss of

meaning and purpose on one level and final regaining of it on another. The loss shows itself in our life situation in doubts and disillusionments about our personal relationships, aims, activities, and ambitions to do with worldly matters.

What preoccupied us and fed our drive in our work now seems tawdry and not worth all this effort. We question its reality and its right to absorb so much of our energy, to demand and receive our concentrated attention. Has it the right to fasten us so securely to the daily grind when God's insistent call to another level of being is there in the background all the time, distracting us?

Of what use is "getting to the top"? Winning that big increase in salary? Being treated with respect and deference as the one who "has it all at her fingertips"? The indispensable manager and organizer? There are times when we ardently want to "throw it all away" because it seems so fatuous. Yet we know we cannot opt out, for we have a spouse, to be faithful to, offspring to put through college, the mortgage to pay off, obligations to associates to fulfill, our own lifelong ambition to bring to its triumphant peak, and a whole life pattern to round off harmoniously.

Somehow we have to learn to live with our growing awareness of it all as a mindless treadmill "full of sound and fury, signifying nothing." In the face of the void, it lacks reality but, nonetheless, must be attended to.

The true reality is an indefinable something located in our inner emptiness. It is drawing us till we want to let go of everything else and recklessly jump into that abyss to meet its embrace.

At this point some people have a breakdown so that circumstances force them to take a long rest from their life-in-the-world obligations and ambitions. Others keep on mechanically, but their hearts are no longer in it, and they feel nothing but relief when someone else replaces them or the time comes for them to retire. This disillusionment and lack of drive registers as a humiliating disaster, yet it may well be a special grace opening the way for us to concentrate on "the one thing necessary."

Alarmingly, the problem increases, rather than diminishes, once we free ourselves enough for such concentration. It is like a slap in the face to discover that we cannot find "meaning" in the things of God either, though we dumbly and idiotically know the meaning is there somewhere, expressed in ancient Egyptian hieroglyphics no doubt. (And no one taught us at school or in the boardroom how to interpret these.)

Faced with the void and its implications, we find ourselves unable to understand God's meaning and purpose in our own lives or those of others. His actions seem arbitrary and often absurd. In fact, a general senselessness defying the rational mind pervades the whole void. We slither aimlessly about, till we remember the lesson about staying still and waiting.

When we apply this perseveringly, we are able to accept that it is no wonder we cannot understand the divine meaning and purpose when it is infinite and eternal, while we ourselves remain time and space imprisoned. It is also perfect love and omniscient wisdom, while we are full of a "lack of love" and a distorted vision.

During the years spent in the void, we slowly learn to rest in peace in God's incomprehensible will, to trust its apparent irrationality, to have faith in its beneficent care of us in and through our life circumstances (even when they appear to be nothing but "a tale told by an idiot"), and to hope doggedly in a future blessed by fulfillment in blissful union with him. Our concept of life's meaning and purpose has changed radically as grace permeated those levels where our basic semi- and unconscious rebellion and misapplied self-will lay hidden but potent.

4. *The Darkness of Entombment.* In the void we are in the process of dying with Christ and being buried with him so that our life may be his life and we be hidden with him in God, our glory part of his (see Col. 2:12; 3:2–4).

When Jesus hung upon the cross, he was in a kind of void between earth and heaven: the vacant space left by total immolation for the sake of others; the blank of utmost loneliness and dereliction expressed through his cry of abandonment and desolation; the kenosis of the God-Man brought about by the complete surrender of his awareness of his Godness, coupled with his immersion in his representative Man-ness; and his slavery as "sin-taker" for us when he himself was sinless.

In various degrees and ways we, his lovers and beloveds, are invited by him to enter into crucifixion and kenosis with him so we may eventually share in the glory of his resurrection. We have to die to self by hanging there with and in him through the sufferings—physical, mental, psychological, emotional, and spiritual—that God permits to come to us and that our own and others' sins and sinfulness bring upon us.

After the crucifixion comes the interlude of the entombment before the resurrection can occur. The sense of entombment is an essential aspect of the void.

If we think of Jesus' corpse lying still, cold, and alone on the stone slab, we shall understand some of the basic elements of the spiritual state of those called to die with him in order to rise with him.

There is the darkness of this stone cavern behind its stone door. No chink of light anywhere. It makes us feel our intellect has been blinded, and we shall never understand anything about God again. Though we carry on with our daily lives more or less satisfactorily, we suffer a kind of sense-deprivation of the spirit. (Only those who have experienced this state of being will find meaning in this paradox.)

One form of torture of prisoners is to lock them into a pitch-dark cell where there is complete sense deprivation so that time ceases to have meaning, as does everything else. Entombed with Jesus, we are in a similar state because all the satisfactions and enjoyments that come to a human being through his senses of hearing, sight, smell, touch, and taste no longer have power either to distract or fulfill us. We have become one-purposed in our longing for God, and the senses cannot tempt us away from it with their promise of surface, ephemeral delights.

Since we have renounced the lesser good for the greater, the Spirit obliges by paradoxically taking away their irrelevant enticements—in a spiritual sense. To express it otherwise, our senses and our bodies and all our material being continue to function adequately for the purposes of everyday life. However, in relation to the spiritual life, we have become numb and dumb to their joys, attractions, and any urge to seek deep meaning and fulfillment through them.

We have been brought to that state where we float in the void of blind faith that none of our senses can affirm as a reality. We gaze upon God without seeing him. We hear his Word without understanding it. We taste his supportive love without any sweetness or consolation—as if our taste buds had been anesthetized.

He is weaning us from all such reassurances by imprisoning us in this void of sense deprivation. He means us to learn how to enter, unencumbered, into the central mystery of his Being, spirit to Spirit.

He has led us into the depths of the night of faith. In it, usually for years after painful years, we learn to lie down with the dead Jesus in the tomb. We learn to lie there patiently and wait in our nakedness. We learn what being still really means as we contemplate the Savior's unbreathing body—not with bodily eyes, but with spiritual ones of unquestioning faith and a love stripped of self-seeking.

We are seeds fallen into the ground and undergoing the hidden metamorphosis from which we shall at last emerge, essentially changed persons, into spiritual resurrection.

5. *Loneliness.* The inner void is a crucifyingly, lonely space of nothingness. We shall probably find there is no one who can understand our state, except one who is also in it or one who has endured it and emerged. The one in it may be able to offer sympathy and sharing. The one emerged can give reassurance, understanding, encouragement, guidance, support, and hope for the future. This is so only if she or he has some understanding of what the lonely one is passing through or has emerged from. Such understanding is rare.

The void can have many guises, including those of mental, emotional, or physical breakdown. It is often mingled with factors associated with these. It adapts itself to whatever needs to be purified in the particular sufferer, since it is always under the control of the Spirit. It is not easy, and almost impossible, to discover a fellow sufferer who is enduring the same searching trial in the same ways.

A qualified, learned, compassionate spiritual guide who has had both personal experience of the void and of supporting others immersed in it is a very special blessing from God—one that is seldom given. An essential part of learning to live at peace in the void's faith dimension is that of being able to trust oneself blindly to the hidden guidance and control of the Spirit coming directly instead of through an intermediary. The purification process includes enduring it alone with God—and an absentee God at that.

The only sure and never-failing companion is Jesus in his passion, especially in Gethsemane and in his cry of dereliction on the cross. We can find here, in union with him, the strength and purpose to endure; to hang helpless and in agony in absurdity; to give oneself up out of love for his redemptive work; to stay with, and in him gladly for love of him, to share his loneliness; and to comfort his desolation.

This is anything but mere sentimentality, as anyone who has really done it knows. It is a genuine, self-obliterating response of "yes" to his questions, "Will you drink of the cup I must drink of?

Will you watch one hour with me? Will you take up your cross and follow me? Will you give yourself with me for others? Will you love my Father's will wholeheartedly as I do to the end? Will you follow me wherever I lead? Will you go down into the darkness and die with me and then wait with me in my tomb till resurrection morning comes? Will you dare Sheol with me?"

If we agree to share his loneliness, we shall indeed be lonely and in that desolation share the essential loneliness of all abandoned, helpless, despised, outcast, comfortless human beings whom he represented on the cross, as well as those lost in the black loneliness of habitual, severing sin or those immured in purgatory in this life or the next.

We may have friends who love and try to comfort us, but this will do little to ease what is a loneliness of our very essence crying out for God. Only if they have been through it themselves will they be able to apply balm.

In the ultimate there is only one who can fill the void of loneliness with genuine fulfillment, and it is God himself. He is busy preparing in us a place fit to receive him. All we can do is wait in faith, hope, and love that feel like unbelief, despair, and a numb indifference that will never be able to love again. "Out of the depths have I cried unto thee, O Lord. Lord, hear my voice!"

6. *Awareness of Sin*. The void strips away inessentials, leaving the emptiness of nothing to cling to but God—and in bare, stubborn faith.

Because the motes in our own eyes (our absorption in the secondaries of created things instead of the one primary necessity of God) have now been removed, at least partly, by grace, we see much better. One of the things we see with our new sight and in startling clarity is the reality of sin.

Not so much actual sins—these are fairly obvious to discern, and we have long ago trained ourselves to watch and guard against them in our own lives. No, what we now see with the eyes of our spirit enlightened by the Spirit is innate sinfulness. We become aware of its substratum in ourselves (those tangled "roots" that I mentioned earlier) and in other human beings we deal with. We helplessly observe it issuing from us and them in all kinds of meanness, envy, prevarication, self-delusion, self-love, and rationalization. Squirming and humiliated, we face, with the help of grace, that, "This is me...that is the person I loved and revered so much." If we do not take care, this pitiless insight will cause discouragement and fear in ourselves, and a judgmental, condemnatory, disillusioned attitude toward others—even cynicism.

The taste of this racial and personal, basic sinfulness is bitter indeed. We want to spit it out and rush to grab something sweet to gourmandize on and hide that vile flavor. We have been living all the time with a despicable traitor within us, and till now we have never even glimpsed him. His cronies are present in all other members of the human race, and from them emanate the sorrows, sins, evils, and disasters of living on this planet that has been tipped off its axis.

Some of the penitential psalms now have for us as never before a cogent, humbling, and intensely personal message. Paraphrasing a little, we cry with St, Paul, "Who will rescue me from this enemy within?" and reply with him, "Nothing else but the grace of God, through Jesus Christ, our Lord."

We know now that we really do need a personal Savior, that we would be lost without Jesus, that an essential part of our void experience is acknowledging our personal, basic sinfulness for which the only cure is the grace that Jesus gives. We cry, "Lord, you came to save me—because I needed you so much. I need you even more now that you have shown me the truth about myself. Only show me what you want of me, and I will do it. I will do anything at all for you, my Lord and my Savior, because you have rescued me in my great need."

This time we really mean it, because we are so much closer to Truth itself. We have been given the grace of a genuine horror of sin because of what it did to Jesus and still does to him suffering in his members. We long to help heal the wound of sin in his body. We offer our personal wound of sin to him, humbly pleading for the grace of healing. As never before we understand the cleansing power and action of grace, sacramentally and otherwise. We hunger for it, seek it, open ourselves wide to receive it. We become beggars for it.

We learn what spiritual poverty really means and again lie down with Jesus in the tomb, content to be naked, trusting in his body and blood to heal us of our grievous wound. We are learning what it means to be dead to self and alive to Christ and his members.

In the inner void the self becomes so tiny in the "All"ness of God. We do not lose our individuality, but we long for it to be absorbed in Christ, so that we become exactly that aspect of his extended incarnation and continuous passion destined for us by the Father.

We pray for deliverance from all evil—for ourselves and for every other human being. We pray fervently, for at last we have "seen" what naked sin and evil are and what they bring about— the death of the Loved One.

7. We Enter a State of Heroic Abandonment and Endurance. Our void has opened up enough for us to receive the grace we must have to enable us to lie down in the Lord in a state of advanced inner stillness, trust, and hope. The void's darkness begins to take on the faint glow of incipient dawn, the intense silence is broken by the first tentative twitterings of birds as something soundlessly rolls away our tomb's stone door.

The sense of being stifled eases, and we draw deep breaths of sweet, cold, dew-drenched air. There is deep within us an awareness of wounds having been healed; of a terrifying emptiness having been filled with Someone; of Love himself annihilating loneliness forever; of a still, silent, crystalline joy, and blessedness welling up from deep, deep down, crying in exultation, "Abba! Alleluia! Amen!"

Then we see a Person walking like a king toward the light growing and glowing every second in the tomb's open doorway. It is as if the light emanates from him, as if he is the light. Wondering and worshiping, we rise from our stone slab, gather about us the new white garment we find there, and follow the Light into the new day. There is no void of inner emptiness anymore. Christ risen and triumphant fills it with himself.

The Certain Stage

I

What is in the empty space?
"Nothing"
I'm sure there's something there
Or someone maybe. It can't just be space.
"It is." I don't believe you.
"Look for yourself."

I looked—and there was the Emptiness
brimming with Presence. "A very present help
in time of trouble."
I told you so
"And now I believe you." It's impossible
that this could be—and yet it is.
I see it, feel it, touch it, sense it,
And yet I neither see nor touch it.
"That is my way at a certain stage—
that emptiness that is the fullness of being."

II

The second tornado came—and I
am right on the cliff edge,
ready to be blown, hurled, out to sea.
Sea? That's the same thing—
limitless, endless, open space.
No one and nothing. "Except you."

I *am* the nothing, the No Thing.
The space which is reality,
The substance, hidden in the accidents.
"I don't understand you."
Yes, you do. Don't think so much—
just be. In me. For me.
Where I am, how I am.

I AM. Be I AM in me.

III

I will clothe you with infinity.
And place you on the ruin of eternity.
Panoramas are too vast
to capture in errant words
or concepts related to time and space.

Floating is the only way to negotiate them.
I will hold your hand and lead you
along vast alleys of nowhere
to the consummation and the peace
that permeate creation where it began.

My vision of reality is through a window
down whose pane it streams in torrents
distorted by everlasting rain—or else
serenely makes an incomprehensible statement—
"This is I. Do not try to understand.
Just be in me."

And so, caught up in mystery
I gaze upon my window pane that cascades
with you and all your mysteries. I bow my head

before your multitudinous Presence that is
a simple statement of reality. "I AM."

One day the rain will cease, and I
will gravitate through you
into an infinite eternity.

IV

My dog
senses the end is near. She stays
close to me—beside my bed at night
at my feet during the day.
                Goodbye
We'll meet again, somewhere, somehow.

Consummation Paradox

"Where are you, my God?"
I seek you all about me and you are not there
And yet you seem to tell me: Here I am. Everywhere.
Nowhere.

I never leave you, but you have to realize
I use disguises. If you persist in seeking me
under that disguise I used a month, a year, ago,
you will be hurt and disappointed. I change, and you must
change with me, or be left alone, bereft, bewildered, lost.

"But why do you do it?" That you may know me better.
You are my Chosen one who must discover me
beneath a multitude of impermanent changes
        of attire and behavior.
I remain myself, absolute, infinity—and close as a lover's kiss.

You have to learn to recognize me. It's hard, I know.
You come running to me—arms outstretched to be enfolded
by what I was to you when the season was different, and you
were ardent and your heart bursting with untried love,
your every gesture and word a lyric, your very speech a poem!
It was beautiful, but it was only the prelude. Now
the flowers have seeded, the petals are all gone, the scent
is blown away on the wind. And yet...

and yet, how beautiful this autumn is!
        The prelude to our consummation
by my death in you, and your resplendent life in me.

The Inflowing of God

Mount Carmel (undated)

The doctrine of the immanence and indwelling of the Trinity is scriptural, especially emphasized by Jesus at the Last Supper. It is also experiential, as any lover of the Lord can testify. That God is within the human heart is a fact the lover is certain of, though he cannot explain how, or accurately locate, the Presence.

God is also transcendent and therefore "out there" in the sense that he permeates and keeps in being the whole of his creation. But for the Christian living his faith daily and in all circumstances, the dynamic fact is that God is "in here," he is "within" me, he inhabits my deepest places, and his fallowing influence pervades me from that hidden sanctuary, for I truly am the temple of the living God.

Those to whom St. John of the Cross addresses his treatise on the night of the spirit already live in constant awareness of the mysterious, compelling, inner Presence. In the log of wood analogy, John presented God as gradually penetrating further and further from the periphery. We can think of "inflowing" in the same way, but if we accept that God is already present through grace in our inner depths, the ground of our being, then it is also true to think of the inflow of God as an upwelling, like artesian waters, from a hidden source, within our own inner fastness. His purpose is to permeate us from where baptism placed him, "here within."

The doctrine of the indwelling of the Trinity is one of the Church's most spiritually compelling and fruitful. In book 2 of his treatise on the dark night, John is examining the way in which this indwelling increases its power and presence till it accomplishes its will to possess us completely, to our own supreme fulfillment and final joy in the third syndrome of light, fulfillment, and joy. We were created to be receptacles of God, just as the ciborium is fashioned and used to hold the hosts, and the chalice the wine. "This night is an inflowing of God into the soul" (*Dark Night* 2:5:1). If we consider the infinite immensity of God and the apparent finiteness of our inner being, it seems impossible that such an inflowing could take place without either shattering us or sending us mad. In fact, if we resist, either of these alternatives is possible.

But if we recall that it is our spirit that God invades and that he himself is pure Spirit and that spirits are of their nature immaterial and boundless, then a different perspective results. We can see the process is like water flowing into water, yet ethereal in a way that water does not permit, for we can touch, see, taste, and even hold water in our cupped hands, but we cannot do any of these with spirit. What does Scripture say about spirit?

Spirit in the Old Testament, originally "wind" and "breath," is conceived as a divine, dynamic entity by which Yahweh accomplishes his ends: it saves, it is a creative and charismatic power, and as an agent of his anger, it is a demonic power.... Spirit is opposed not to the material (for which there is no Hebrew word) but to flesh—the mortal, corruptible, weak, and sinful element in man. Spirit is not flesh (McKenzie, *Dictionary of the Bible*, 841–842).

In the New Testament (see McKenzie, 842–845), the concept of spirit is varied and greatly enriched. The Spirit is the mysterious, saving power of God, and it authenticates Jesus as Messiah. The growth of the Church is the work of the spirit, who empowers the disciples to be witnesses to the resurrection. The Spirit manifests itself through various charismatic phenomena, and it is given to the whole body of believers; it is a divine, dynamic force.

In Paul's writings, the spirit pervades Jesus and his Mystical Body, the Church. The risen Lord exists in the spirit, not the flesh, and the Spirit frees from sin and death. The Spirit is the creative, life-giving force present in the risen Jesus and through him in the Church, and it makes them both the temple of its indwelling, praying in them, sanctifying them, distributing gifts, bestowing salvation. The believer knows; understands; has faith, hope, and charity; only through and in the Spirit. The Spirit stands in antithesis to the flesh, which is both the law and the tendency to sin; there is in the believer a conflict between flesh and spirit—between the principle of corruption and of eternal life. John's gospel stresses the Spirit as Paraclete (helper) and Spirit of truth. The words of Jesus, which are the revelation of God, are spirit and life. The Spirit is a stream of life for the believer; it enables the apostles to remove sin. The Spirit is sent by the Father, and by Jesus, remaining forever and revealing the true reality of Jesus.

Pondering the above, we see how wide and deep is the Spirit's influence and power in the spiritual realm of our lives. If we think of our inner purgation as the work of the Holy Spirit, which it is, for he is the Sanctifier, we shall find it easier to disencumber ourselves from limiting concepts of time, space, and as bodies of flesh destined for corruption. We shall gain a perspective in which eternity and infinity are seen as realities and in which our spirits are seen as immortal and therefore partaking of eternity and infinity now. The mystery of the inflowing of God into or up through the soul, though not intellectually understood, will become acceptable in faith.

The inflowing *can* happen. It *does* happen. By means of it, "God secretly teaches the soul and instructs it in perfection of love, without its doing anything, or understanding of what manner is this infused contemplation" (*Dark Night* 2:5:1). The secrecy is because the divine action occurs in those deeply hidden recesses of the unconscious, which our human understanding cannot reach and in a way it cannot grasp. Spirit infuses divine love into spirit, which remains passively receptive—this receptivity being a positive act of our will to remain open to God no matter what. "Not doing anything" is, paradoxically, a concentrated willingness to "let God do it." His doing comes about in a blind stirring of love in thick darkness. Why he does what he does, we cannot know. How he accomplishes his ends, we cannot understand. All we can grasp is that God's action *is*. As contemplation deepens, this reality becomes a basic fact and experience in our spiritual lives.

In the active nights and the passive dark night of sense, we have already done all we could through our own deliberate efforts, aided by grace, to clear out of God's way all that could impede his inflowing. The rubbish gone and the channel opened, we have now to leave the regulation of the living water to him. He will also deal with the embedded detritus still in places clogging the bed of the stream and with the roots of the trees impeding the flow along its banks, here and there. At times our spirit is able to receive the action and invasion of the divine Spirit in tranquility. But mostly, John warns us, it experiences "affliction and torment."

The soul's state is like that of a foreigner in a strange land who knows nothing of the language, yet is aware that for his very survival, he must somehow understand what the wise and would-be helpful inhabitants are doing their best to communicate to him. Their tongue has no similarity at all to his own, either when spoken or written. Its speakers avoid all "body language" that might provide him with clues; more and more the conviction grows in him that he is severed from everything or everyone to do with his own native land—all familiarity, comfort, companionship, and intercommunication—in fact, all that means and recalls "home." He is an exile who will never be able to go home again, for all routes back have been blocked by a cataclysmic earthquake—the eruption of the divine into his inner depths. Of course he suffers; at times, atrociously. His only recourse is to submit and blindly trust these incomprehensible but kindly intentioned strangers, hoping that someday, sometime, they and he will understand one another.

It is the "height of Divine Wisdom, which transcends the talent of the soul" that causes it to suffer during this inflowing, as does also the growing awareness of "its [own] vileness and impurity" (*Dark Night* 2:5:2) revealed in contrast to the beauty and purity of the enlightening Spirit. So we have inability to comprehend on one level, coupled with an only too exact comprehension on another level. What a clash and discord! What war between "two contraries"! "The natural strength of the intellect is transcended and overwhelmed by [this] great supernatural light" (*Dark Night* 2:5:3).

The impact of the collision of the divine Sinlessness with human sinfulness produces other effects on our inner being that overflow into mind, emotions, and body. We feel enmity between ourselves and God as if there were a life and death battle going on and we were in imminent danger of being annihilated by a force as mighty as a nuclear holocaust. We feel fear, dread of destruction, and pitiful longing to be spared. Peter cried, "Depart from me, O Lord, for I am a sinful man!" For the first time we truly experience Peter's dilemma, and the full reality of being embedded in the fallen human race, with no possible rescuer except the divine and sinless Savior. We are ready to cry out with Gerard Manley Hopkins:

> But ah, but O thou terrible, why wouldst thou rude on me.
> Thy wring-world right foot rock? lay a lion limb against
>   me? scan
> With darksome devouring eyes my bruised bones? and fan
> O in turns of tempest, me heaped there; me frantic
>   to avoid thee and flee?

To experience God as an implacable enemy, who crushes one underfoot, while he gazes with merciless all-seeing eyes upon the wreckage that was once our proud inviolable, complacent selves, is truly to become frantic to flee. The psalmist experienced the same dread and defeat:

> You have plunged me into the bottom of the pit,
>   into the dark abyss,

> Upon me your wrath lies heavy,
> And with all your billows you overwhelm me....
> My only friend is darkness. (Ps. 88)

This is one of the passion psalms. It foretells the plight of Jesus dying on the cross under the fearsome load of the world's sin and the feeling that even God had abandoned him because of the inevitable recoil of sinlessness when he had permitted himself to "become sin for our sakes." Jesus on the cross is our refuge in our own spiritual trial, uniting our anguish with his is our way to sanity and hope.

God's purpose in letting his love register on us as dire enmity is, as Hopkins goes on to say, "That my chaff might fly; my grain lie, sheer and clear."

It is to strip us of our hidden pride by showing us the truth about ourselves, that we are "unworthy of God or of any creature" (*Dark Night* 2:5:5), who thought ourselves well on the way to being canonized, and much further up the *nada* path than anyone we knew, or graciously compared ourselves with. Now, in our grim self-knowledge of our "evils and miseries," we cannot see how we can ever overcome or escape or be cleansed from them. God permits this experience of helplessness so that we shall have no other solution but to turn to his mercy and love, claiming in faith what he has promised us: "Come unto me all you who are heavy-laden, and I will refresh you." The hand that smites is also the hand that heals. In fact, the very smiting is an essential part of the healing process, as the surgical analogy reveals.

At other times, when the inflowing is strong, we experience ourselves "as if beneath some immense and dark load" (*Dark Night* 2:5:6). This is because God's invasion has reached a degree of forcefulness that cannot be deflected; his presence is thrusting in upon us deep down in the ground of our being, and we are as yet too spiritually weak either to withstand or receive it. This is the effect of what John calls "substantial touches." These are the caresses of Love registering directly upon the inner substance of the soul—Spirit to spirit. Until we have become other Christs in transforming union, we may experience such a divine touch as a kind of crushing under the heel of a giant.

> A thing of great wonder and pity is it that the soul's weakness and impurity should now be so great that, though the hand of God is of itself so light and gentle, the soul should now feel it to be so heavy and so contrary, though it neither weighs it down nor rests upon it, but only touches it, and that mercifully, since he does this in order to grant the soul favors and not to chastise it. (*Dark Night* 2:5:7)

God's desire to possess our spirits completely is as importunate as any passionate lover's on the fleshly level. Because this inflowing has passed far beyond the outer self and the senses and is thrusting in toward the furthest recesses of our being—the bottom of the inner abyss, the most secret, deepest strata of our psyches where no one has ever reached before, let alone touched us—we are both terrified and appalled. If this can happen to us, anything can happen. There is no refuge left, nowhere to flee or to hide.

> Where could I go to escape your spirit?
> Where could I flee from your presence?
> If I climb the heavens, you are there,
> There, too, if I lie in Sheol. (Ps. 139:7–8)

We are indeed in Sheol, and he is indeed there. And what is he doing? He is "stripping [us] of the habitual affections and attachments of the old man, to which [we are] very closely united, knit together and conformed" (*Dark Night* 2:6:1).

"Affections and attachments" are the equivalent of "addictions." An addiction is something or someone we are quite unable to give up through willpower alone. Think of the alcoholic who is impotent against his hated addiction until he acknowledges his helplessness and deliberately submits to a "Higher Power." Think of the fanatically obsessed lovers who are ready to wreck others' lives and their own if only they can be together and satisfy their addiction. Their compulsion is a kind of emotional devouring of each other, yet they are convinced it is the noblest of loves, excusing the drastic betrayal of other loyalties, if only they can satisfy their mutual craving. Or think of the workaholic, the sportaholic, the drug addict—anyone with a magnificent (or debasing) obsession or compulsion to use others in some way or other while sincerely professing the sublimest of motives, all the need, loves, the do-or-die fanaticisms, the my-country-right-or-wrong blindnesses—together with the extensive, devious rationalizations twined around them like well-established, clinging ivy. Think of these only too common habitual mechanisms of human living, loving, and being, and you have some idea of what John so accurately diagnoses to be there in our depths, running our lives for us.

They are all part of the "old man," the racial entity we are born into and cannot escape from except by grace, the first sin-suffering, evil syndrome clamped on us that only the second, love-suffering prayer can dislodge. "United, knit together, conformed...." We are one with this old man through both heredity (racial and personal) and environment. We are so much one with him that we are knit together. We can no more be unraveled from him and his influence than one colored wool thread can be abstracted from the pattern it makes with the other colors, without destroying the whole garment. We are conformed to the old man within, molded by our immersion in humanity, so that we let him express himself as he wishes through us, using us to repeat his patterns over and over and over again. (Think of the repetitive patterns of world history, let alone those of the individual.)

Seeing all this by divine revelation, Paul cried out, "I do those things I don't want to do, and what I want to do, I don't do. Who will deliver me from the body of this death [i.e., the old man]?" He answered himself, "Nothing else but the grace of our Lord Jesus

Christ!" Paul was enduring the inflowing of the ray of divine, darkness revealing to him his human plight and his only remedy for it—the redeeming, renewing graces bestowed by Jesus through the penetration of his Spirit. We are imprisoned in "this sepulcher of dark death [of the old man]...until the spiritual resurrection which we hope for" (*Dark Night* 2:6:1).

We have to die on one level before we can be reborn on another. The grain of wheat has to fall into the ground and change radically or it cannot bear fruit. "The sepulcher of dark death" is the place where we face both God and ourselves and see the disparity. Because our faith, hope, and love have already been purified to some degree by our earlier struggles and purgings, and contemplation has been established, though imperfectly, in us, we are able, even though in such sore trials, to cling to hope. As we are now so closely one with the suffering Lord and his death, we have, deep within us, the indestructible certainty that one day, when God is ready, we shall rise with him. But before that, we must be entombed with him, becoming entirely passive, while the Spirit works his miracle of transformation in us.

Death and Rebirth

It takes a long time to die.
You are dying even while
you are learning how to come alive and be.

On its bed of nails, inert,
lies what will be the corpse,
or else it wanders mesmerized in circles
tremulously fingering familiar objects,
dazed, entangled in confusion,
clawed at by ancient, rooted agonies
persistently invading spaces
up till now inviolate from their raids.

Seeking relief, it stumbles back to bed,
curls in the fetal posture, instinctively assured
such small exposure of its surfaces
will mean less piercing of their vulnerabilities.
It lies there cradling its omnivorous pain
arms crossed protectively on breast
knees hunched to meet them—
a tightly rolled up ball of dread
hoping to be invincible when most at risk.

At last, enfeebled into acquiescence,
it yields to the invaders, accepts defeat,
and, face to wall, it dies.

Your old self lies there like the husk
from which the butterfly has just emerged.

You seem to rest and sleep. You dream...

Teresa's transformed silkworm spreads
its iridescent wings set free to soar
in palpitating life. It settles
on a gleaming flower and sucks its honey.
Cocoons are now forgotten. This liberation
intoxicates, infusing such huge torrents
of new life it almost shudders it apart.
The safe confinement of the husk is gone for ever.
Tremendous gales may come to tear its wings
yet in its carefree joy it takes no heed
of that or any other threat.

> You have become this butterfly.
> You live and soar and have your being
> in him who is your home. And never
> will you die that death again, for though
> it was the end, through it you were reborn.

The Prayer of Stupidity in the Dark Night

Review for Religious (November/December 1991)

There are two transition phases in the spiritual and prayer life of the committed, faithful Christian who gives more than adequate time to prayer and constantly seeks and does God's will, motivated by love. The first is the passage from meditation to contemplation in the dark night of sense. The second occurs in the dark night of the spirit as we approach full union.

In John of the Cross's terminology, those who practice discursive prayer and meditation are "beginners," those who have been given the initial grace of contemplation are "proficients," and those who have attained full union through submitting to the passive purifications of what he calls the dark night of sense and spirit are the "perfect." The perfect are in that state of oneness with the Trinity, variously called transforming union, spiritual marriage, the seventh mansion, the fullness of the indwelling. They have passed through purgatory in this life.

One of the main sufferings of purgatory is the intense longing for God, coupled with just as intense an experience of his absence, even of having been spurned by him. There is also an acute awareness of the sinfulness, impotence, and inadequacy within us that is holding us back from the promised fulfillments of the heavenly state. The purgatorial sufferings of the dark night of the spirit also have these characteristics.

219

In the spiritual life, initial generous commitment to God and his will, plus faithful prayer in some form of structured meditation, usually results in consolations that are warm, sweet, joyful, and emotionally satisfying. These give us a sense of God's presence. When, maybe suddenly, we are deprived of all such comforting and reassuring experiences, the shock is severe. Now there is darkness instead of light, aridity instead of sweetness, a cold heart instead of a warm one, a hunger and thirst for an absentee God replaces our former joyful, consoling sense of his presence. Where before we were borne along in his loving arms, now we trudge. This is a crisis point of great significance to our future spiritual development or lack of it. We are being given the choice either of throwing everything up and opting for a life of outwardness and lack of struggle with ourselves and God or of clinging to him in faith and obstinately keeping on through years of trial and suffering, often severe.

He is an absentee God now, one whom we cannot reach and who seems to have forgotten us. Our stripped-bare faith, hope, and love idiotically keep on affirming he is still there, closer to us than breath, only our former recording apparatus is now nonfunctional. We cannot feel him at all—except as our enemy. All we have to offer God now are various forms of what I call the "prayer of stupidity." We are unable to feel or believe that what we are experiencing is the beginning of contemplation, defined by John of the Cross as "nothing else than a secret and peaceful and loving inflow of God" (*Dark Night* 1:10:6). God himself is infusing love and grace into us, but, as yet, we remain defective receiving instruments, scarcely in running order. The purpose of the passive nights is to correct our inadequacies and remove all obstacles to God's "peaceful and loving inflow" so that we can be made fundamentally one with him and be the perfect vehicle of his grace for others.

Elsewhere John writes of "tearing down rather than building up" in his "instructions for advancing in contemplative union with

God." The senses and faculties have to "be left behind and in silence, so that God himself may effect the divine union in the soul. As a result, one has to follow this method of disencumbering, emptying and depriving.... The soul must journey by knowing God through what he is not, rather than through what he is.... We must...raise it above...all distinct knowledge and apprehensible possession to supreme hope in the incomprehensible God" (*Ascent* 3:2:1–3). Traditionally this has been called the apophatic way. The "prayer of stupidity" is inseparable from it but can and does lead to the heights of union with the Trinity, if we remain staunch.

Now it is as if he has walked out on us in indifference, absenting himself to some unplotted planet, gone on an indefinite vacation and leaving both letters and telephone unanswered: "Yahweh, hear my voice as I cry! Pity me! Answer me! My heart has said of you, 'Seek his face.' Yahweh, I do seek your face; do not hide your face from me" (Ps. 27:7–9). We are still very far from the heights.

The "prayer of stupidity" has become our daily, habitual state. We are in the night of faith but cannot believe we are, should any knowledgeable person tell us so. Spiritually we compare ourselves to a deaf mute who understands almost nothing of the wonders of creation and cannot express even the little he does grasp—or to one of those poor handicapped persons who must be mothered and led round all their lives, or to someone who has been kept forcibly awake for days on end, or taken on a long march, or reduced to exhausted numbness by some superhuman physical task. This is what we feel. Logical thought about our state does not seem possible. We are unable to react. We feel embalmed. We are utterly impotent.

The "prayer of impotence" is helpless suffering. It is as though our heart's load of love has become a lump of concrete that no effort can lift or even budge an inch. The result is frustration. We want to pray, but no words come. We want to move that love, but it lies, lead-heavy, on the heart, incapable of response. "Lift up your hearts?" It is impossible. Now we are tempted to discouragement, self-pity, introspection, and feverish attempts to become absorbed in external activity and showy good works. The remedy, we slowly learn, does not lie in physical activity, though a gentle walk taken in order to praise God in the beauty and intricacy of his creation may do much to lift the weight from the heart and calm the soul. The remedy lies in relating our state to that of Jesus and abandoning ourselves to the Father with him.

When was he impotent? In the first place, he chose to become impotent when he chose to become incarnate. As the Son of Man, he limited himself and laid aside the almighty powers of the Son of God. Though from time to time these were demonstrated in miracles and in events such as the transfiguration, the power was always circumscribed and temporary. To be truly human, he had to let himself be afflicted by impotence. He felt it as he saw the apparent triumph of evil, the hardness of people's hearts, the guile and power of the Pharisees, the obtuseness of the chosen people, the silliness of the apostles, the self-seeking of even those closest to him.

He chose to be impotent because he chose to leave us free to align ourselves with either good or evil. In some places he could not work miracles because of the unbelief of the people. He willed to be dependent for his power upon our faith or lack of it. This meant that often he found no way of expressing the weight of love crushing down upon his heart.

In the hour of darkness, the only way he could do this was by submitting to evil, letting the powers of night have their temporary way with him. His chosen impotence became total in his passion, crucifixion, and death. Here he demonstrated to us that at its deepest levels, impotence can be creative, for the will that is one with God's always has some power to choose. Its restriction is real, yet it is still free to choose God's will as presented to it in the form of darkness and negation. In this way impotence is made positive by means of the "prayer of amen." In Gethsemane, Jesus, pleading and impotent—in the grip of human fear—longing to be spared and rescued, could yet nullify his powerlessness by telling the Father, "Nevertheless, not my will but yours be done." In this way the prayer of impotence can be transformed into one perpetual amen. "Amen, my God, to all you do, and permit, and will. Amen. Amen."

The psalmist says, "And all the world is filled with his glory. Amen. Amen." When the prayer of impotence is transmuted into the prayer of amen, the glory of God envelops the whole of creation, including the mute, interior darkness within us. It is a glory where clouds and darkness are about his face, but it remains glory, just as there was glory in the shadowy garden when the total submission of Jesus caused an angel to come with a chalice of comfort. Comfort will also come to us when united with Jesus in his prayer of impotence. Grace will strengthen our will to endure and will soften it so it can more readily receive the imprint of God's will. The "prayer of amen" recognizes God's sovereignty and that we belong to him. The angel of comfort sent to us helps us to pray with Jesus, "Do with me what you will. I belong to you."

We have now entered the "prayer of deep abandonment." When we seem incapable of accomplishing anything, spiritually speaking, we can yet offer this prayer. It is always possible to surrender ourselves to God, no matter what the situation. Paradoxically, abandonment becomes easier when any kind of effective human action has become impossible.

Everywhere and in everything, the will of God works incessantly to bring about good through the vast, interlocking network of cause and effect. Only good, in the end, can come to us out of that intricate work of love the Father performs through the Son in order to rescue us from the crippling effects of sin.

Though we seem lost in the desert like the Israelites, that desert is in fact the embrace of God, the showing forth of his will. It is the way to the Promised Land of full loving union with him. It is a foretaste (without taste or with only a bitter one) of the fullness of joys promised those who renounce all for love of him.

To say amen continually in the desert, to abandon ourselves to his actions and will, in whatever form they present themselves, is to exercise faith, and at times heroic faith. To affirm the existence and tender care of a heavenly Father who seems to have removed himself finally, to trust him who gives no sign of his presence, to continue to offer ourselves to a Creator we are tempted to think has discarded us, is paradoxically to come closer to him at every moment. This is so even if we have no feeling of that closeness. The prayer of self-abandonment would not be granted us unless God was not already living, moving, and loving there within us. The grace to cling in bare faith to this fact has already been given us.

Reverence for what the present moment brings results in peace. The will that rests in abandonment and loving trust in God's will, whatever happens, cannot be troubled. Our Lord's gift to it is his peace, that peace which is not what the world gives, but his own. It bestows sweetness in the midst of bitter, unalleviated aridity. When no words or holy thoughts will come, when no love will rise in the heart, the will can yet abandon itself to God's will, and that is prayer, even if we can call it nothing but the prayer of stupidity.

And so we arrive at the "prayer of driftwood." Everything is so obscure, God's ways are so incomprehensible, arbitrary, inconsistent, and absurd. His darkness is so enveloping, and our minds are so confused that his will seems like one of those implacable currents that have the power to bear a craft across vast stretches of ocean. We have become a piece of driftwood that can do nothing but let itself be carried along in this current's force toward some unknown and unforeseen landfall. God's ways are inscrutable, but all-loving and all-wise.

Therefore, to trust oneself to the current of his will (expressed in the events, circumstances, duties, trials, and inspirations of each moment) in this blindly unquestioning manner is to acknowledge that he has the right to dispose of us in whatever way he chooses. It is to admit being a chattel, a slave, even in one sense a thing, though endowed with reason, free will, and an immortal soul.

Let go, and let God. Let be, and let him act. When we float in the "prayer of driftwood," this current of his will can become so effortless that it brings joy—the kind of joy we do not feel but are certain is there, a joy that is spiritual and independent of the emotions.

To vary the theme, we could call this the "prayer of Jesus sleeping in the boat." St. Thérèse, who spent most of her mature spiritual life in dark insensibility, remarked once, "Jesus, as ever, sleeps in my little boat." Her one concern was not to waken him by making any agitated appeals to him. He slept. But he was there. Why then should she fear? When the tempest arose about the sleeping Lord, the terrified disciples roused him, and in an instant he quelled the waves and winds with one command. Thérèse willed to trust him so much that she could let him sleep even though the tempest was raging within her and the boat of her life was being tossed about in its turmoil. It was no matter—Jesus was there. Deep within her, he held her fast and safe in his arms.

There is no need to rouse the sleeping Lord with cries for help and demands for comfort. As long as we do our best to steer our own boat, despite all spiritual tempests, in the direction of God's will, Jesus, asleep or awake, will do the rest. "Why art thou affrighted, O my soul? And why art thou downcast? Trust in God." The Lord who permits the tempest will not let our frail craft perish in it.

Such childlike confidence in God flows from that poverty of spirit Jesus affirmed as blessed. No one lives as firmly in the sacrament of the present moment as a little child, and no one clings to her father so trustingly in a storm. If we are like this, we are one with Mary in her fiat. This is the "yes," the "I take everything" prayer, the "let it be done unto me according to your word" prayer.

In this prayer, we do our best to submit to everything, to repudiate nothing. Even as we wince, we give God all that he demands. We say humbly, "Yes Lord. Certainly, Lord. Anything else, Lord?" With Mary we consent to bear the Christ child, however long and arduous the labor. God's loving care will support us until we can bring him forth and his Father can look on us and proclaim, "This is my beloved son—or daughter—in whom I am well pleased."

We affirm that, by this bringing forth of Jesus into our life situation, we are helping to strengthen his Mystical Body and continue his redemptive work in the world. By constantly living in the fiat prayer, we present him to others as the Light that shines in the darkness, theirs and ours, the one who influences them silently by his grace when they are not even aware of his action. Blind and dumb ourselves, we yet show him forth in each action of the day done for love, in every moment in which we say yes to God's will as it is presented to us. The least action motivated by pure love, says John of the Cross, is worth immeasurably more than mighty acts done without love. In the fiat prayer we strive to accept everything for love, cooperate with grace because of love, consent to bear Christ as a labor of love.

Our prayer has now become the "prayer of hidden oblation and silent offering." Jesus' whole life was one of hidden oblation. The most extraordinary of human beings lived the most ordinary of lives for thirty years. When he said, "Behold, I come to do your will," he agreed to a hidden oblation that would culminate in the kenosis of the cross, where every aspect of his divinity and his power to redeem the world would be concealed behind outward humiliation, impotence, and degradation.

The mother of this son consented in simplicity and quiet dignity to the same extremes of oblation, as her heart was crucified at the foot of the cross. She offered herself. She offered her son. As Vatican II affirmed, "in a wholly singular way she cooperated by her obedience, faith, hope, and burning charity in the work of the Savior...." But others, too, who live out the prayer of hidden oblation participate in the Lord's work. In this prayer we unobtrusively take up our cross daily and follow him. We permit ourselves to be crucified with him in a thousand unobtrusive, humiliating ways, believing trustfully that we shall rise again into glory with him.

This prayer understands enough of the mystery of redemption to long to be part of it. We receive the courage and strength to practice it through the daily offering and reception of the Eucharist, our food for the journey into kenosis with Jesus, his hidden oblation and silent offering there for us in the host. Love and suffering become so intermingled within us and in our lives, so much a part of our prayer as to be inseparable, once our own hidden oblation becomes more and more comprehensive. Yet our spiritual work is done without dramatics and mostly in silent obscurity, as Mary's was.

To give is the incessant need of those who learn and live this prayer. They have heard that Word, which was made flesh, say to them personally, "Greater love has no man than this, that he lay down his life for his friends," and they have replied, "Here am I, Lord. Use me."

The "prayer of hidden oblation" is such a laying down of life, such an outpouring of the greatest love each person is capable of. And so the "prayer of stupidity" has evolved into the "prayer of sacrificial love," through which union with Love himself is attained in the unending joy of the Lord, and not just for the one who sacrifices but for countless others as well.

John of the Cross's *Dark Night,* books 1 and 2, follows through this development of the "prayer of stupidity" using different analogies and terms. *The Living Flame of Love* depicts its fulfillment. This is the "prayer of total abandonment" by which the world is changed, and though few seem to reach its fullness in this life, anyone who sincerely wishes to be! Christ now in the world, as

Vatican II exhorted us to be, must aim at it. Those contemporary Christs who do reach this kind of prayer will be the instruments of God through whom history is redirected and the secular order renewed. They, rather than scientific discoveries or the reorganization of the world's food resources, are the hope of civilization, for through them Christ pours into the world those graces and enlightenments that will inspire people to do what is good, right, and effective for the rescue of our planet from its manifold plights.

Dilemma

Now you've arrived at last, what's it like?
A huge emptiness filled with Christ.
That's a contradiction.
Yes. It's a paradox. What it is is indefinable.
It transcends words and concepts in its "Is"ness.
It's outside human experience, in this world, and on this earth.
It slides away from your mind like water over a weir.
It flows and is gone. It's there, and then it isn't
and yet—it never goes. It IS.
The "Is"ness of a reality that's indefinable.
You're talking nonsense.
You're right—for it *is* "no sense."
Not "sense" as we humans conceive of it.
Not logical, definable, fixed—
a cozy concept you can handle,
gaze at with incredulity and amazement as "just right,"
file away, sure it will be there when you want and need to use it.
It's not...
Not what?
Not anything. As we know things.
How can you describe it then?
You can't. It doesn't fit in with human concepts.
All you can do is approximate and know
it's slipped through your fingers like water.
You can't hold it, possess it, clutch it—
it's there and yet it's never there—
not where you can say, "Ah, at last I've got you!
At last I'm holding you and you can't get away!"
It's already gone.
Then, how...?

I don't know. It's all a mystery.
Mystery IS. You can't dissect it, label it, confine it in little boxes.

It's 4 A.M. and we're not getting anywhere.
Maybe you're not meant to.
Then how can I know?
What *can* you know? The human equipment
is unable to contain such infinite knowledge. You can't know.
All you can do is acknowledge the "Is"ness accepting humbly,
conceding that it's beyond you and words
are not the right tools to deal with it.
But you're using words! They're all I have.
I must keep on trying till I grasp something
some shred of the truth—some concept that is exact—
that I haven't made up—that IS.
Maybe it's a hopeless task.
Maybe it is. But I have to try
and I won't give up.

Silent Stillness

In the silent stillness
the still silence rises—
a multitude of tiny silver bubbles
effervescing upward from a hidden spring.

There is light too. Not harsh
upon the vigil-weary eyes
but soft. Smoothly it permeates
every hidden crevice and shines upon
each ravaged, earthquake-wrenched, rock strata.

This light transforms the landscape.
Silence and stillness blend, become
a visionary space astir with shimmering presences,
each one a source of blessedness, an emanation
from that hidden, unplumbed Source
of all-that-is, a subterranean sun
that penetrates all darknesses
with uncreated, unquenched radiance.

Here it is safe to walk, safe
to taste whatever food is offered
and then to eat your fill. You may
lie down anywhere in peace, and sleep—
no nightmares will wrench open
ancient wounds.
        All have been healed
immersed in silent stillness, permeated by this light,
transformed into holy vessels
through which grace cascades unchecked.

Living the End
of My Journey

THE TORNADO

Letter to a Friend (early 1993)

I was peacefully minding my own business in the middle of the night and "resting in God" and giving Jesus my heart, when what I came to think of as "a tornado" got inside my head. No pain. Just a huge turbulence and sense of helplessness. I've often enough told God he "can do what he likes with me, for I belong to him." Well on that night he apparently did! I aged ten years visibly—I don't care about the "looks" part of it, but I do miss my memory. Its loss affects me in all kinds of ways. And, as well, the tumor killed the balance nerve on my left-hand side, so I lurch all over the place like a drunk and periodically fall over—and it hurts! Yesterday evening I took my dog for a walk (or wavering lurch) and suddenly fell backward over the curb onto the concrete footpath. I hit my head, of course, and hurt my whole body, as concrete is unyielding.

Luckily, I've kept my acute sense of humor. I make a lot of good-humored jokes about me and my condition, but I don't really care. I'm ready when God's ready to receive me. He's cagey about that one, and the ironic part is that it is now, when I'm incapacitated through no fault of mine, that he's getting my writing a lot of attention. I can't answer the letters that I receive from readers. I can't answer the questions coherently—and it all exhausts me even more, so mostly I just put it aside. If I can, I write a brief letter and maybe a poem. Poetry is about the only thing I'm writing now. Mostly it comes in the middle of the night as if being dictated. And it's all "dark night" stuff, though in no way is it theoretical and analytical. It just tells how it is—kenosis stuff.

⚶ Enough of this. I've written it because your letter showed genuine interest in me. Briefly, I've always loved solitude and silence. As soon as lay people could be consecrated hermits, I knew it was for me. I wrote to our bishop and he said, "yes," he'd come to my place and consecrate me there—on 30 November 1988 to be precise. It's brought me many blessings. I also live under a private vow of chastity and celibacy made around 1960—frequently renewed before a priest or our bishop. I was "married" in a kind of way (civil, but not a Church wedding). "If it didn't turn out a success, we'd separate." It was not a success, though we had three children, and we both love them dearly. We had a legal separation, and later there was a Church annulment—so I've never been really married to anyone but Jesus, which is the way I want it.

Hope this detailed letter answers your queries. I have a dear friend who does my typing, and I'll get her to take off a typed copy and several xeroxes of this. Then I don't have to go through it all again each time someone inquires. I can tell you are genuinely interested, and that's why I've done a coherent record for you. I suggest you ask ICS Publications what books of mine are in print.

I have a lot of separate articles, poems, etc., in various periodicals, of which I have some copies. Probably they aren't available now. The copies I have are to go in what people call "the archives," which I find amusing.

I'm seventy-one and my health is failing fast. I live on a sickness benefit, plus age pension. Luckily, I own my own home and live in it, rent-free, on my middle daughter's large property. There are ten grandchildren from my three daughters. Long stories there.

I spend most of my time alone with Jesus, resting in him, reading a bit (can't concentrate), contemplating the totaras (a huge New Zealand native tree). I might enclose a poem or two.

Lovingly in Jesus,

Barbara

The Sickbed

A sickbed is a seemly place to meet the Lord.
He likes to encounter chosen ones and find
them resting and receptive, quietly expectant,
unoccupied, alone, attentive but relaxed,
aware immediately of his Presence, and fully there.

A sickbed in its isolation and its silence
is a place of assignation with the One
who occupied himself so often healing
and laying on his hands to soothe and bless.
Lying here, I register his Presence, and I wait.

A sickbed then becomes a prie-dieu and a pew.
Outside ring the birds' clear, dawn-inspired trills.
The totaras rest unstirred by wind or breeze,
their mighty trunks and boughs in dignified repose.
I gaze at them and find his everlasting strength.

A sickbed is a place of symbiosis
Where new effort and exhaustion interfuse—
a heady mixture poured into a scoured dish
now borne to some eternal haven and safe house.
None can harm me now, protected by your heart
          and folded in your arms.

"Turn me, O Lord, and I shall be turned."
You are the master craftsman who restores
fine, old masterpieces and battered artifacts.
You polish off the scratch marks, fit new handles,
empty all the drawers, refilling them with treasures beyond price.

I pray you: Fill me with yourself and crown me
with your everlasting love. Enfold me
and protect me next your mighty heart. Keep me safe
within this citadel of peace and graced repose.
Here is where the refuge is, here the well of love.

Lost Memory

My memory is going...going...almost gone....

It slides away like water on a weir
or sand upon a sandhill in the wind
or thoughts within my mind I try to muster
around another idea for a poem.
Evanescent, unreliable, slippery as wet pebbles
they slip through the crevices in my memory,
dive into the caverns of the unconscious,
and so are lost to me—save that I have a general sense
of jewels sliding from my fingers, too sleek
and capricious to be held, too precious and unique
to be shut up within that jewel case
with all the other heterogeneous treasures.

I am bereft. Where can I find
the jewels that reflected for me
the translucent messages you taught me? I tried
my best to hold them, for they were precious, but
you claimed the repossession of them, telling me
I was not ready yet to grasp their secrets,
hold their sacred messages in my heart
or understand the onerous implications for myself.

And so I sit here helpless in the lowest class of all
Having seen reflections of your holiness, held out my hands,
I see them trickle through and so be lost to me,
save for the elusive memories that haunt and taunt me now.

I Await Your Coming

Here I sit
hand folded in quiescent hand
tranquil where miles of empty beach
yearn for your promised visit.

I await your coming
the rains and flowers that accompany you
making the burnished desert glow
and softening contours as if by gentle mist.

Then as I sit and wait
the knowledge comes to me that you
yourself are drought and dew
both emptiness and overflowing fullness
Kenosis and consummation all in one.

Time to Be Gone

This little, withered, winter's leaf of woman
(hands almost translucent, delicate bones
fragile as crystal) is ready to relinquish
skin's envelope, as meager flesh shrinks to nothing.

These fingers' delicate tendrils
this leaf-woman's symbols of departure
remind me of last autumn in my garden
good-byes everywhere, final farewells,
and yet no grief and no regrets, instead
a tranquil letting go, a freedom to be gone
floating in acquiescence to the season's will
certain of rebirth and metamorphosis
a transformation into kenotic rest in Christ.

70s

It's just about all over now, Lord,
and the gate's already open.
I'm here—waiting. You haven't
come round the bend in the road yet
but you will. My bags are packed
and anything I do now
is irrelevant
unless related to that gate...

So many gates—closed, open, left ajar,
banged shut in my face—
gates to be climbed over or through,
unlocked and then closed carefully behind me—
or nonchalantly left swinging
to slam itself in the wind.

Gates that closed for ever
with a cataclysmic slam.
Others opening to reveal vast panoramas
promising fulfillment if I choose
to climb that ever-steepening hill—
the rising sun's vast rays now tipping it...

None of my equipment spread
between my foot-soles and the crown
of my too often errant brain
agrees that such huge effort
is still at my disposal.

"Lord!"
I cry. "It isn't possible.
I'm far too old!" "Use these," he says,
and tosses at my arthritic feet
a pair of eagle's wings. "Dare you,"
he taunts, "to make the final stage with these!"

Progenitors

This is our last resting place—
unless, of course, you change your mind again!

It's over thirty years since we moved in together.
We've had our ups and downs—I don't deny it—
but, oh, the splendor of those days and weeks
when love's transfiguration glorified the commonplace!

I believe we had some children—"thousands,"
Frank once said, amazed. But I have never
even glimpsed a single one.
I've let you use me any way you liked to bring them forth,
but never did you let me cradle any one of them against my heart.
You are so jealous. You'll not have my gypsy heart
distracted from you for a single hour.
When I ask you where and who our children are,
you smile so fondly at me, kiss my eyes and say,
"Beloved, they are in the best of care. Later on,
I promise you will see and love them all, and you,
my precious one, will be their crowned delight."

I'm old now. Bearing all those children
has drained my strength. But if you lean above me
with your eyes all dark with love, and say, between our kisses,
"I still have work for you. Will you be mother to some more?"
I'll smile and tell you, "You know I can't deny you anything.
Just use me any way you wish. I'll never refuse
to make more children with you, then bring them forth,
until I lie cold in my coffin. Then, glorying in you,
face to face forever, together we will carry on the work
until the folding up of time releases us from such sweet labor.

An Afterword

Barbara was my mother's closest friend from their school days in our northern New Zealand township until my mother's death in 1990. As a child I was aware that Barbara was facing challenges that my family considered extreme. Sometimes it seemed that the odds were too heavily stacked against her, and I remember early on sensing that mysterious forces were at work in her life. After years of a close adult relationship, I know that to have been a life pattern. From her earliest days, Barbara has been called on to draw deeply on her personal and spiritual resources to cope with life and to survive. I am not surprised, therefore, by the wisdom and maturity of her writing, by the insight and the faith she shows in her work, or even by its practical good sense.

As a psychotherapist, what intrigues me when I reflect on her long, lonely journey is the absence of cynicism in her writing and the innocence and spontaneity of her poetry. The spirit of truth pervading her life and work seems ever fresh and simple, and yet I know it to be the result of much research, analysis, and scrutiny.

My professional field overlaps with Barbara's intense interest in and knowledge of psychology. We spend many hours exploring the intertwining of our learnings and the implications for our lives and work. Her never-failing sense of fun and puckish humor lighten our discussions: her incisive wit has not lost its edge over the years. She retains the power to startle with her frank honesty and sudden penetrating laughter.

Barbara has had a profound effect on my life. She has been a valued spiritual guide and mentor. She has met me in the exploration of my own spiritual mysticism with depth, with acceptance, with knowledge, and with wisdom.

It is a privilege to be asked to write this afterword. I feel that I speak not only for myself but for my mother and many others.

Gillian Bowie
Auckland, New Zealand, February 1995

[Untitled]

(Upon the death of Gillian Bowie's mother)

You left us in such unexpected haste
no time to say goodbye or even wave a hand.
We woke and you were gone, and more
in a far land, the whole world's curve away.
You did not know yourself that you had gone
into another realm of light and airiness
having cast off from moorings in the flesh
you were afloat in ecstasy, translated into spirit.

But we were left behind imprisoned here on earth
and could not watch you go, bending at your bed
engrossed in long farewells that eased the wrench,
the tearing out of intertwining roots
of tentacles of loving interaction
suddenly gone slack, incapable
of holding us together.

You left us—
and yet you stay for ever.

Bibliography

Caussade, Jean-Pierre de. *On Prayer.* Translated by Algar
   Thorald. 2nd revised edition. Springfield, Ill.:
   Templegate, 1949.

*The Complete Works of Saint John of the Cross, Doctor of the
   Church.* 3 volumes. Translated and edited by E.
   Allison Peers. Westminster, Md.: Newman Press, 1953.

The Complete Works of Saint Teresa of Jesus. Translated and
   edited by E. Allison Peers. Volume 1. New York: Sheed
   & Ward, 1946.

Doherty, Catherine de Hueck. *Poustinia.* Notre Dame, Ind.:
   Ave Maria Press, 1975.

Furlong, Monica. *Merton: A Biography.* New York: Harper &
   Row, 1980.

McKenzie, John L. *Dictionary of the Bible.* Milwaukee: Bruce
   Publishing, 1965.

Philipon, M. M. *Spiritual Writings of Sr. Elizabeth of the
   Trinity.* New York: P. J. Kenedy & Sons, 1963.

Poems of Gerard Manley Hopkins. Oxford: Oxford University
   Press, 1931.